Sports Illustrated

WOMEN'S GYMNASTICS 2:
The Vaulting, Balance Beam, and Uneven Parallel Bars Events

THE SPORTS ILLUSTRATED LIBRARY

BOOKS ON TEAM SPORTS

Baseball
Basketball
Curling: Techniques
 and Strategy

Football: Defense
Football: Offense
Football: Quarterback
Ice Hockey

Pitching
Soccer
Volleyball

BOOKS ON INDIVIDUAL SPORTS

Badminton
*Bowling
Fly Fishing
Golf
Handball
Horseback Riding
Judo
*Racquetball
*Running for Women

Skiing
Squash
Table Tennis
*Tennis
Track: Field Events
Track: Running Events
*Women's Gymnastics 1
 The Floor Exercise
 Event

*Women's Gymnastics 2
 The Vaulting, Balance
 Beam, and Uneven
 Parallel Bars Events
Wrestling

BOOKS ON WATER SPORTS

Powerboating
*Scuba Diving
Skin Diving and Snorkeling

Small Boat Sailing
Swimming and Diving

SPECIAL BOOKS

*Backpacking
Dog Training

Safe Driving
Training with Weights

*EXPANDED FORMAT

Sports Illustrated

WOMEN'S GYMNASTICS 2:
The Vaulting, Balance Beam, and Uneven Parallel Bars Events

by Don Tonry with Barbara Tonry

Illustrations by Don Tonry

LIPPINCOTT & CROWELL, PUBLISHERS
New York

FIRST EDITION

Designed by Linda Dingler

Library of Congress Cataloging in Publication Data

Tonry, Don.
    Sports illustrated women's gymnastics.
    (The Sports illustrated library)
    CONTENTS: v. 1. The floor exercise event.—
v. 2. The vaulting, balance beam, and uneven parallel bars events.
    1. Gymnastics for women—Collected works.
I. Tonry, Barbara, joint author. II. Title.
III. Title: Women's gymnastics.
GV464.T62   796.4'1   79-25050
ISBN 0-690-01908-4 (v. 1)
ISBN 0-690-01907-6 (v. 1) pbk.
ISBN 0-690-01909-2 (v. 2)
ISBN 0-690-01906-8 (v. 2) pbk.

80 81 82 83 84 10 9 8 7 6 5 4 3 2 1

Contents

3. Uneven Parallel Bars   157

Introduction

This book teaches the female gymnast how to perform in three gymnastic events: vaulting, balance beam, and uneven parallel bars. It is a sequel to *Sports Illustrated Women's Gymnastics 1: The Floor Exercise Event,* which provides a general introduction to gymnastic training and offers instruction in the tumbling, acrobatic, and dance skills featured in the floor exercise event. The four events discussed in the two books comprise the women's Olympic Gymnastics All-Around Program.

In both books, the skills are rated from 1 (elementary) to 10 (advanced) to indicate the approximate degree of difficulty for each. This rating system is intended to guide the gymnast and coach in choosing the skills best suited to the performer's particular level of expertise. Beginners, of course, should learn the simpler skills before proceeding to the more difficult ones.

An attempt has been made to present accurate, instructionally sound descriptions and illustrations of the most common skills in each event. *In some cases the illustration does not demonstrate the most fundamental skill pattern (for beginners) or technically perfect form (for advanced performers), and thus differs somewhat from the descrip-*

tion in the text. This is because most of the illustrations are based on films of champions in action during competition. The films were studied for hundreds of hours before segments were chosen and committed to the drawing board. The overhead projection method was used in drawing the skills featured in both books, which together contain more than 400 illustrations and over 2,000 individual figures.

Prerequisites for most basic skills are specified; these should be mastered before the performer begins practicing the skill. By noting the prerequisites and the difficulty rating of a particular skill, the gymnast and her coach can determine whether or not she is ready to attempt it.

Spotting methods for many skills are described so that coaches will know how to proceed in physically assisting the performer and assuring her safety.

In some cases, variations of basic skills are included. Usually, these are not discussed as fully as most basic skills because they resemble the basic versions in most respects, and are illustrated. However, when a variation is significantly different from or more difficult than the basic skill, it is given a more detailed description.

Sports Illustrated

WOMEN'S GYMNASTICS 2:
The Vaulting, Balance Beam, and Uneven Parallel Bars Events

1

Vaulting Brief History

The history of horse vaulting stretches back in
time to early civilization. Perhaps the oldest sur-
viving illustrations of "animal jumping," created
two thousand years before Christ, are to be found
on the island of Crete off the coast of Greece.
These wall paintings depict exhibitions similar to
the rodeo, with men being thrown onto or jumping from the back of a bull, and in the process
performing what appears to be a handspring
movement with support from the bull's horns.
Thus modern-day horse vaulting is a gymnastic
event that derives from ancient cultures in which
advanced techniques of mounting and dismounting from steeds were practiced.

In 1911, Frederick Jahn, considered the
founder of modern gymnastics, developed and
popularized routines on the pommel horse in Germany, with an emphasis on swinging and turning
movements rather than vaulting. Eventually,
vaulting techniques were taught throughout
Europe as various "gymnastic systems" emerged.

At one time, women's competitive vaulting
featured a high springboard, pommels, and a
much higher horse than is used today. As time

13

d, the pommels were removed to eliminate hand placement restrictions
the present measurements and requirements were standardized throughout
world.

Safety

Safety measures are very important when learning vaulting skills. If injured,
you will not only waste valuable training time while recuperating, but will
probably also lose some of your strength and overall conditioning.

Excessive repetition in vaulting often causes shin splints, which can be
extremely painful. Shin splints are pains in the front of the lower leg that you
feel when you run and jump from the vaulting board. Eliminating this potential
problem requires limiting the workout to only a few vaults, at first. On your
first day of vaulting, from ten to fifteen jumps off the board after a running start
is plenty. Increase this number very slowly over the course of several weeks.
As a general rule, twenty vaults are about all you should perform in any
workout. It is also wise to give your legs a day's rest between vaulting sessions,
and to pay attention to the condition of your legs from day to day. The best
remedy for shin splints is rest.

Consider that a falling body moves at a rate of thirty-two feet per second.
This factor, coupled with forward momentum and rotation (sometimes around
two axes—somersault and twist), makes the landing technique absolutely vital
to the safety of the vaulter. Special attention must be given to landing in a fairly
upright position with knees and hips flexed to lessen the shock on impact. The
landing area should be flat and heavily matted.

Finally, be sure that you are spotted (physically assisted) whenever you are
learning a new vault.

General Vaulting Technique

Vaulting is a running and jumping event characterized by very aggressive action
for a short period of time. Like diving, it requires close attention to the small
details of approach, takeoff, good form, and landing.

The vaulter's ability to concentrate on a vault is influenced by how comfortable and consistent she is in her approach and takeoff. The distance between
the starting point of the run and the vaulting board should be measured, and
the length of the running strides should be the same on every approach so that
the feet are consistently brought down on the board at the right place without
the need to break stride. The hurdle (the jump onto the board) should be low

and short to maintain the power built up during the run. The takeoff (the jump off the board) must be done with the correct arm lift to achieve proper elevation. The performer should land with slightly bent knees to absorb the impact following the descent.

As with other gymnastic events, the beginning vaulter must learn these fundamentals before proceeding to practice the skills. The following drill, performed using the vaulting board and landing mats but without the horse, will teach you the correct procedure for the hurdle and landing.

Hurdle and Landing Drill

Practice jumping from one foot to two feet from a stand just to the rear of the vaulting board. Your legs and hips should not bend excessively during your jump onto the board. Attempt to execute a fast bouncing movement that springs you into free flight. Follow through with a leg push by extending your ankles, knees, and hips as completely as possible as your feet leave the board. Lift your arms forward-upward with each jump. Practice tightening your buttocks and keeping your legs together in flight to maintain good form and a tight body position. Bend your hips and knees as the landing occurs and attempt to "stick" the landing so that no additional steps must be taken to maintain your balance. Be sure to land on a well-matted area.

This drill should be done frequently. The rate at which your vaulting ability improves will be determined by how often you practice the drill, and by how rigorously you comply with the instructions in the more complete discussion of vaulting techniques that follows.

Hurdle and Landing Drill

The Run

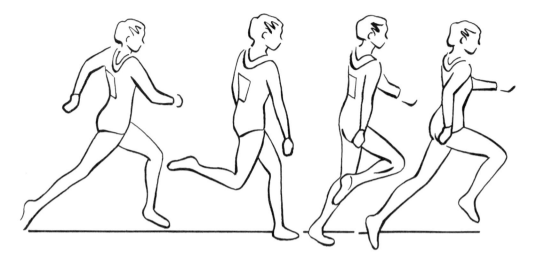

Basic Vaulting Techniques

The Run

Stand a short distance (about twenty feet) from the vaulting board and mark your starting point. Run to the board, hurdle (*see* below) onto it, and spring into the air. Repeat this several times. Always start the run with the same foot and do not hop or change the length of your stride to accommodate the board. Find the correct starting point for an even, natural run by beginning the run slightly behind or in front of your original mark until your steps and hurdle are consistently comfortable. Your run should be an easy, arm-swinging type with normal strides. A beginner should practice the run, hurdle, and takeoff —landing on a crash mat—until she can consistently perform them correctly.

After practicing the short run, start as far back as the rules allow (about twenty meters) and repeat the procedure to master the approach from this distance.

The Eyes

Watch the board until you are ten or fifteen feet from the jump. Then raise your eyes to the vaulting surface (horse, mats, table, etc.) so that you can jump with confidence. If you do not look at the horse until after the jump off the board,

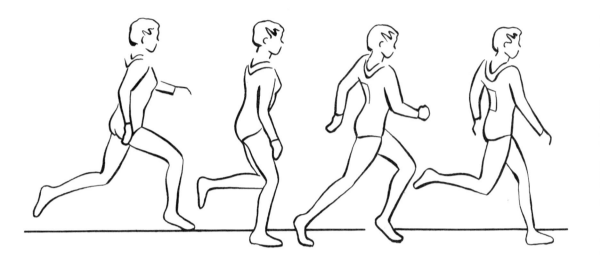

you will not have enough time to "feel yourself" performing the vault. You should develop this inner feeling (vision) for the ensuing vault as you approach the horse.

The Hurdle

The hurdle (the jump from one foot to two feet for the takeoff) should be an *extension of the run.* Keep it relatively *low* and *comfortably short;* if you jump too high or too long, you will lose power. As you jump off the board, your arms should help you lift—a good jump requires careful coordination between arms and legs. Hold your arms behind your hips and raise them forward-upward as you take off. This arm position may be modified slightly as long as your arms are used to help you lift. Study the arm positions in the two illustrations that follow.

Hurdle With Basic Arm Lift

As you jump from one foot to two feet, your arms are placed next to your hips and start lifting forward-upward before the takeoff.

18

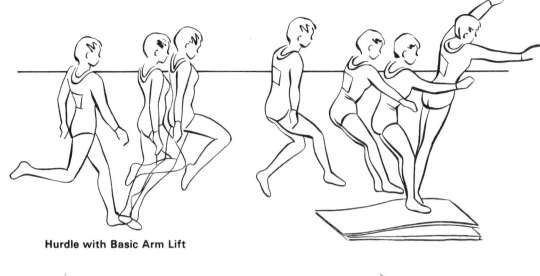

Hurdle with Basic Arm Lift

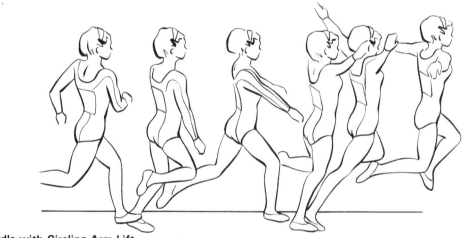

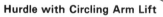

Hurdle with Circling Arm Lift

Takeoff

Hurdle With Circling Arm Lift

Your arms move sideways-upward as you take your last step before the hurdle. As you jump from one foot to two feet, your arms complete the circle and lift forward-upward before the takeoff. This style emphasizes the arm lift but leaves the arms in a slightly lower lifting position than the basic arm lift as the takeoff occurs.

The Takeoff

Land on the board with your center of gravity (hips) slightly behind your point of support (feet). The faster you run, the more you will have to allow for this factor. The knees and hips progressively straighten during the jump from the board. This is a very fast movement that requires lots of practice.

20

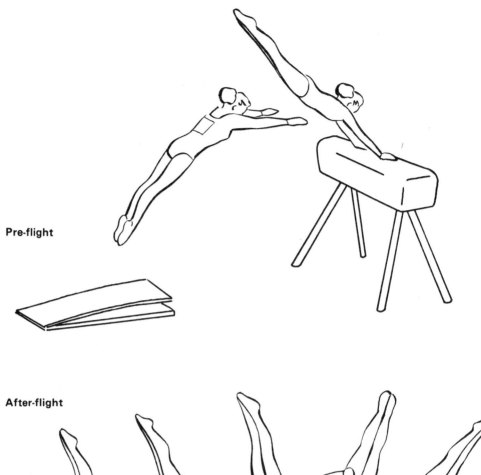

Pre-flight

After-flight

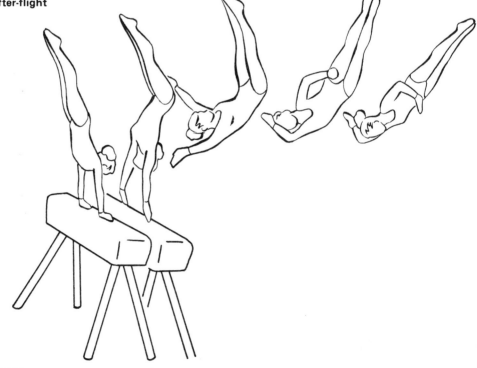

Pre-flight

Pre-flight is the phase of the vault that begins after the takeoff from the board and ends with the push off the horse. As your vaulting and confidence improve, move the board farther away from the horse. The general rule here is: Place the board as close as necessary to allow you to attain the required free pre-flight position. If your vault becomes weak because the board is too far from the horse, it must be moved closer so that you can develop sufficient elevation and distance after pushing off from the horse. One characteristic of a poor vault is that it "dies" on the horse. Inexperienced vaulters very often make the mistake of equating maximum pre-flight distance with good vaulting technique.

After-flight

After-flight includes all movement following the push off the horse through the landing. A strong after-flight with good elevation and distance results from a powerful jump off the board, arm and shoulder push off the horse, and correct body alignment. In general, handspring-type vaults should be performed with complete extension in all joint areas as the hands leave the horse; exceptions are the Yamashita and forward one and a half somersault vaults, which are usually executed with an early piking and/or tucking action as the push occurs. Body extension (layout) before landing is required on all vaults except one and a half somersault vaults, exempted because of the obvious difficulty of complet-

ing the somersault high enough to execute a layout before landing. Some vaults, such as the cartwheel and handspring, have built-in extension. Other vaults (squat, stoop, and straddle) require a fast body extension prior to the landing.

The preceding illustration serves as an example of after-flight technique. It is an advanced skill and should not be attempted until the prerequisite skills are learned. The performer pushes off the horse directly into a piked position. The early pike allows the gymnast to begin the twist early, using the opening action from the pike to initiate the twist (cat twist) and thus completing the full twist sooner than she would have otherwise.

Landing

The legs act as shock absorbers and should flex with every landing. Land as erect as possible, flexing your knees slightly or more deeply depending on the force and elevation of the vault. A ninety-degree angle at the knee joint is considered enough bend to absorb the shock of the most forceful landings. Ideally you should land with both legs together; however, it is better to keep them slightly apart if lateral stability might be sacrificed. Try to avoid taking an extra step or two to maintain your balance after you land. Arms should be

Landing

held almost vertically overhead upon landing or they will be jarred out of position by the impact. Practice your landing technique by jumping off elevated surfaces often. Carefully study the arm positions (motions) in the illustrations in this chapter.

Following is a summary of basic vaulting techniques.

Start
- Measure distance for consistency
- Begin with same foot each time
- Eyes on vaulting board
- Coordinate arm swing and leg step
- Even strides with pumping arm motion

Run
- Build up an amount of speed suitable to your vaulting ability
- Eyes off board and focused on horse

Hurdle
- Low, short hurdle with little knee bending
- Fast leg extension with arm lift

Pre-flight
- Assume correct pre-flight angle for vault
- Push off horse by extending or flexing appropriate body joints

After-flight
- Extend hips before landing

Landing
- Land with knees slightly bent and eyes on mat

VAULTING SKILLS

After practicing the basics, you are more or less ready to apply them to vaulting skills. Learn the squat stand, squat, straddle, and stoop vaults first. These vaults are excellent preparation for the handspring-type vaults. Always work with a spotter and use good-quality landing mats.

Jump to Squat Stand Vault

Skill Level 1

Practice this skill until all phases are well coordinated.

Basic Description

(1-3) After a short run or fast walk, hurdle and jump to a squat stand, placing hands on the horse and bringing both knees between arms.

(4) Push with legs to jump from the horse. Stretch (but do not arch) body during the descent, and extend arms obliquely upward.

Remember, land with knees slightly bent to absorb the shock, and try to avoid taking any extra steps to catch your balance.

Prerequisites

Jump to a squat stand on the floor from a push-up position. Correct approach and takeoff from the board.

Jump to Squat Stand Vault

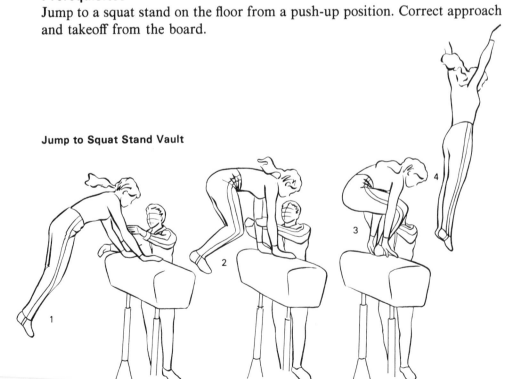

Spotting

Stand on the side and in front of the horse and stabilize performer by grasping her upper arm as her hands contact the horse. Hold arm and place other hand on performer's stomach during the landing.

Squat Vault

Skill Level 1

With the help of a spotter, inexperienced vaulters should begin practicing this skill with the vaulting board placed close to the horse, and assume a squat position rather than an extended body position immediately after the jump from the board. The ability to straighten the body before touching the horse will come with practice, and the board can be moved back for this purpose as the performer develops confidence.

Basic Description

(1) Run and hurdle.

(2-3) Jump and reach for the horse. Contact the horse with hips extended and shoulders stretched. Push downward toward hips with arms, bring knees toward chest (maximum bend), and watch the horse until shoulders pass over it. As the push is initiated, keep toes pointed.

(4-5) After hips pass over the horse, quickly extend body and raise arms from hip area to a rear-upward position overhead.

(6) Land with slightly bent knees.

Squat Vault

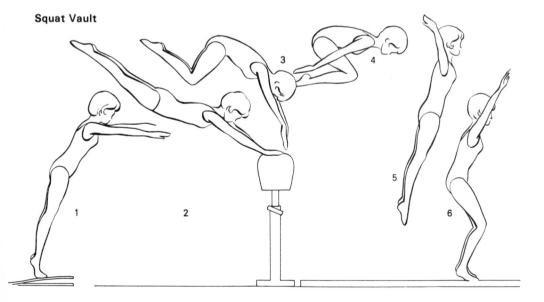

Prerequisites

From a push-up position, jump vigorously to a squat stand. Jump to a squat stand on the horse.

Spotting

Hold performer's arm throughout vault. Some spotters prefer to stand directly in front of the horse facing the performer as takeoff occurs. In this case, grasp both upper arms and step backward as performer lands.

Spotting the Squat Vault

Straddle Vault

Skill Level 1

Beginners usually straddle their legs and bend their hips immediately after the jump from the board in their first attempts to perform this vault. As performer improves, the board should be placed farther back to provide room to improve the straight-body, pre-flight position.

Basic Description

(1) Run, hurdle, and reach for the horse.

(2) Contact the horse with hips extended and shoulders stretched. The upper arms and upper body should form a nearly straight line.

(3-4) Push downward (with rounded back) toward hips forcefully with arms. At the same time, pike-straddle legs forward. Keep eyes on the horse until the push is completed.
(5) Extend hips and join legs.
(6) Land with slightly bent knees.

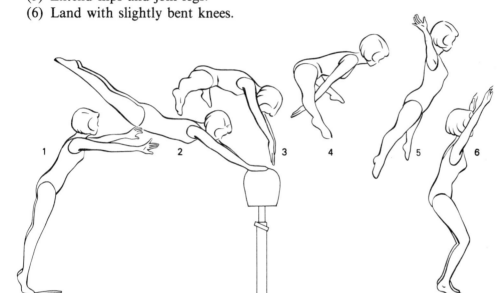

Straddle Vault

Prerequisites

Jump to a straddle stand on the floor from a push-up position. Jump to a straddle stand on the horse, as illustrated.

Jump to Straddle Stand on the Horse

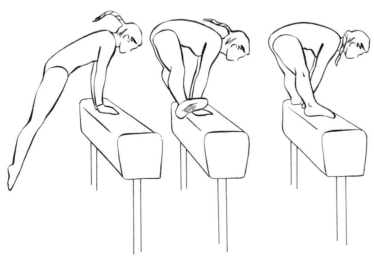

Spotting

Stand directly in front of performer. As performer touches the horse, grasp upper arms, step backward, and assist the landing. The beginning performer may fail to clear the horse with her feet; always be ready for this possibility.

Spotting the Straddle Vault

Stoop Vault

Skill Level 3

This vault should be done aggressively. It requires lots of push and a fair amount of flexibility.

Basic Description

(1) Jump and reach for the horse.

(2) Contact the horse with hips extended and shoulders stretched. The upper arms and upper body should form a nearly straight line.

(3) Push downward forcefully (with back rounded) and elevate (pike) hips. Keep legs straight and joined. Watch the horse to insure follow-through action with arms and back.

(4-5) Bring legs between arms, and extend hips as legs pass beyond horse. The arms move downward-backward-upward after the push.

(6) Land with slightly bent knees.

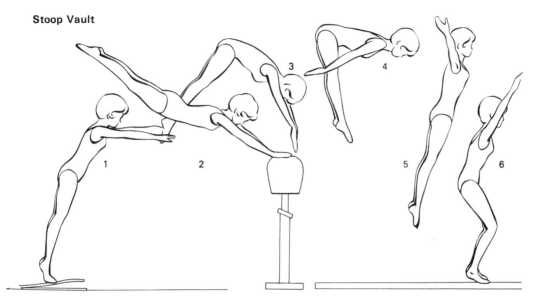

Prerequisites

Stoop to a stand from a push-up position on the floor. Squat vault.

Spotting

See squat vault. Quickly grasp performer's upper arm as her hands push off the horse. Move in the direction of the vault and assist the landing.

Spotting the Stoop Vault

Forward Handspring Vault

Skill Level 5

Forward handspring vaults are quite different from stoop, straddle, and squat vaults. The latter require a reversal of rotational motion as the hands push down on the horse, while handsprings continue the original rotation pattern from beginning to end.

Almost all continuous-rotation vaults have a "blind spot." (The cartwheel is an exception.) This means that during some phase of after-flight, the performer must depend on "feel" for orientation. The blind spot of a forward handspring occurs as the body passes through the inverted position.

Learn the handspring by first practicing the pre-flight phase on a broad, matted surface such as a trampoline, with assistance from spotters. By the time you are ready to practice this and other inverted vaults, you should have a good jumping technique and be comfortable in a handstand position. Be sure you can safely recover from the handstand after your spotters get you up there!

Practice the last phase of handspring-type vaults by kicking or bouncing from a mat, trampoline, or other surface through the inverted position and onto a soft landing area. Be sure you are spotted carefully until you are perfectly consistent. However, keep in mind that you must gradually end your dependence on physical assistance from a spotter if you hope to develop confidence and become self-reliant.

The handspring is probably the most abused vault in gymnastics. Many beginners attempt this vault prematurely, before they have had enough vaulting experience, because it represents "big time" vaulting. Good form and technique are often lost in the process.

Basic Description

A good gymnast keeps her hip muscles tight and rotates with a straight body. The head is tilted forward very subtly in the after-flight phase so that the performer can watch the mat during the landing.

(1) Jump with the board far enough from the horse to allow body to rotate in a layout to a handstand position. (There is no pike except during the takeoff.)

(2) Contact the horse in a handstand position. This position may be somewhat lower if performer has powerful pre-flight momentum. A slight

angle between upper arms and upper body is desirable for extension in the shoulders during the push-off.

(3-4) Extend all joint areas during the push-off. Do not pull head and shoulders forward during flight in anticipation of the landing.

(5-6) Land with arms obliquely overhead and with knees slightly bent.

Forward Handspring Vault

Prerequisites

Handspring on the floor. Jump to a handstand on a broad surface such as a trampoline.

Spotting

Two spotters are necessary during initial attempts to perform this vault. One spotter stands directly in front of vaulter between the board and the horse, the other on the far side of the horse. The first spotter lifts vaulter's hips into a handstand position; the second supports performer's lower back and grasps upper arm. Guide gymnast to a soft landing on the mat. If the pre-flight phase is very consistent, one spotter may stand on the far side of the horse to spot the after-flight only. Grasp performer early and support her all the way to the landing mat. A good spotter also regulates performer's rotation.

Spotting the Forward Handspring Vault

Cartwheel Quarter Turn Vault

Skill Level 5

Basic Description
In the quarter turn vault, the twist is initiated from the push off the horse by pulling the shoulder of the right arm to the right and looking to the right.

(1) Jump as if to perform a handspring with a slight shoulder twist. Most beginners start twisting much too early and fail to get enough handspring rotation.

(2-3) Execute the quarter turn while reaching for the horse with both hands.

(4-5) The second hand should contact the horse almost immediately after first hand touches. Push with both hands simultaneously as body approaches a vertical position.

(6) Extend shoulders and spine as much as possible when pushing off and begin another quarter twist.

(7-9) Land with arms obliquely overhead and knees slightly bent.

Cartwheel Quarter Turn Vault

36

Prerequisites

Cartwheel quarter turn on an elevated surface such as a trampoline. Cartwheel quarter turn *from* an elevated surface. Handspring. (The plain cartwheel vault, usually considered a prerequisite to learning the cartwheel quarter turn vault, has been omitted because the sideways landing can be hazardous to the knee joints.)

Spotting

A beginner should have two spotters. One spotter stands in front of the horse to lift hips for pre-flight. The other spotter stands behind the horse to grasp performer's waist during the after-flight phase. If performer's pre-flight is consistently correct, only one spotter standing on the far side of the horse is necessary.

Half Twist on—Half Twist off Vault

Skill Level 6

The performer must be drilled on the correct twisting direction before trying this vault. The two half twists equal a full twist in one direction.

Basic Description

(1-3) Jump as if to perform a cartwheel vault, but turn head and shoulders under to add another quarter twist.

(4) The right hand will invariably contact the horse just before left hand does. The turn should be completed with body slightly behind (below) the vertical handstand position.

(5-8) Push off vigorously with both arms and stretch shoulders and spine. The after-flight push should help to initiate the second half twist: As push occurs, pull left shoulder backward into the twist and turn head under left upper arm. Try to keep body very straight during the last half twist; any bending of hips will retard the twist.

(9-10) Land with knees slightly bent and arms held obliquely overhead.

If the left hand is put down first on the initial half twist (round-off style), the after-flight half twist should be to the right.

Prerequisites

Round-off over the horse. Handspring over the horse. Practice the twist from a handstand on the floor, landing on your back on a crash mat, or from an elevated platform, landing on your feet on a crash mat.

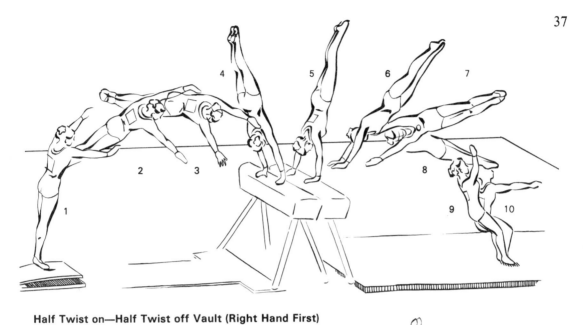

Half Twist on—Half Twist off Vault (Right Hand First)

Half Twist on—Half Twist off Vault (Left Hand First)

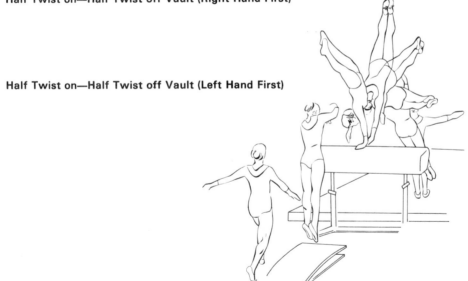

Spotting

Two spotters are advisable when this skill is being learned. One spotter stands in front to guide hips during pre-flight; the other stands on the far side to support performer's back during the final twist.

Yamashita (Piked Handspring) Vault

Skill Level 5

Basic Description

(1-3) *See* the forward handspring vault for the pre-flight phase. The pre-flight position at the moment of contact may be slightly lower than usual because the piking action during the after-flight phase affords easier rotation.

(4-7) Push out in shoulders forcefully as hands contact the horse. Pike by bringing upper body toward legs. The legs tend to stall as the pike occurs. Keep thigh muscles tight.

(8-9) Shoot legs forward by extending hips for an early hip extension before landing.

(10-11) Land with knees slightly flexed and arms held obliquely overhead.

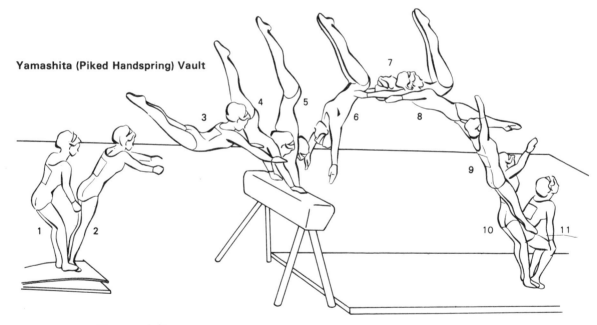

Yamashita (Piked Handspring) Vault

Prerequisites

Forward handspring vault. Kick to a handspring and pike to a sit on a soft mat. Attempt a piked handspring vault onto the trampoline. Kick or jump from a trampoline into a piked handspring movement with a spotter supporting the landing.

Spotting
See forward handspring vault. Grasp performer's upper arm and lower back as hand-push occurs and provide support during the landing.

Yamashita with Half Twist Vault

Skill Level 6

In this skill, a shallow piked position is assumed and the half twist (cat twist) is initiated during the opening from the pike.

Basic Description
(1-2) *See* the forward handspring vault for the pre-flight procedure.
  (3) Watch legs as you pike.
(4-5) Shoot legs forward; pull right shoulder and arm to the right; turn head to the right and under right upper arm; bring left arm to the right across chest; twist hips right.
  (6) You should have enough forward rotation from the jump and push to land in an erect position.

Yamashita with Half Twist Vault

40

Prerequisites

Forward handspring vault. Yamashita. Piked forward somersault with a half twist on the trampoline is recommended.

Spotting

See spotting instructions for forward handspring vault. The spotter may stand on performer's left side, support upper back, and assist the twist by spinning performer in the direction of the twist.

Yamashita with Full Twist Vault

Skill Level 8

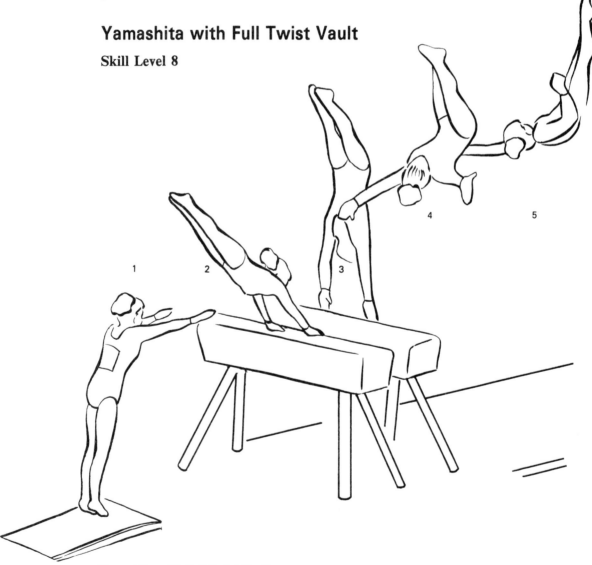

Yamashita with Full Twist Vault

Basic Description

(1-2) Jump off the board and contact the horse at approximately forty-five degrees below the vertical handstand position. Keep body straight.

(3-4) Immediately push with arms and shoulders into a right angle piked position, spread arms to the sides, and (very important) focus eyes on feet.

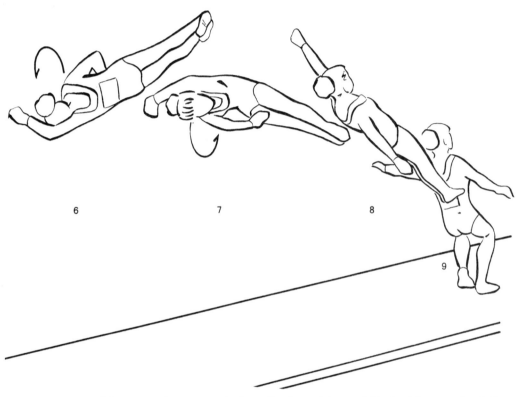

(5-7) Quickly shoot legs out of the piked position while looking under left armpit toward the floor. Your left arm moves behind head and right arm is pulled in close to body to the left. Your hips are turned to the left as the piked position is opened. Execute the full twist in one continuous motion until you see the final phase about to occur. The head should lead the twist so that your eyes can tell you where you are.

(8-9) As you sense the landing approaching, extend arms to the sides to slow down the twist. Land with slightly bent knees and hips.

Prerequisites

Yamashita vault. Yamashita half twist vault to an erect standing position. Piked front somersault with a full twist on the trampoline recommended.

Spotting

Stand to the left of performer on the mat side. Support performer's lower back during the Yamashita (pike). As the twist is wrapped, remove hands and quickly support performer's upper back during the last half twist and the landing.

Forward Handspring with Full Twist Vault

Skill Level 8

Two methods are currently used to perform a handspring with a full twist. One method requires a slightly piked (back rounded) position that is initiated immediately after the hand-push (*see* illustration for the forward handspring vault). A fast extension from this slight pike coupled with movement of the arms from a wide position to a close-to-the-body position creates twisting force. This technique is a modification of the standard method used for the twist in a Yamashita with a full twist.

The second method, illustrated here, utilizes the surface of the horse to initiate the twist. This is done by pushing off the horse with a slight hip turn in the direction of the twist, followed by a shortening of the radius of rotation on the body's twisting axis (bringing the arms to the mid-line of the body). This method requires the performer to clearly leave the horse (complete the push-off) with only a subtle hint of a twist that is almost unobservable. Beginners have a strong tendency to hold the horse with one hand and twist too much before leaving the horse. This tendency can be avoided only by mastering the basic forward handspring movement with a flighty push-off action.

Basic Description

See the forward handspring vault for the pre-flight phase.

(1-3) Extend in shoulders. Watch the front of your body as you leave the horse with back rounded slightly. Pull right shoulder to the right. Notice that performer in the illustration has pushed into a slight hip twist to the right before bringing arms toward the mid-line of her body for the fast wrapping of the twist. This is the performer's method of initiating the twisting action from the horse.

(4-7) Turn head to the right and under right upper arm. Bring left arm across chest to the right. The closer arms are to vertical axis of the body (spinal column), the easier the twist will be.

(8) Bend knees slightly for the landing. The arms should be extended to the sides prior to landing to slow the twist.

Forward Handspring with Full Twist Vault

Prerequisites

Excellent forward handspring vault. A full twist executed from a handspring on the floor to a landing on your back on a heavily matted area.

Spotting
Stand on the far end, right side. Reach under the back and allow performer to roll a half twist onto your arm after the push-off. Move behind performer and support the last part of the twist and the landing.

Hecht Vault

Skill Level 7

The hecht is different from all other vaults. It requires a relatively low pre-flight position, an exceptional reach, and reversal of rotation in a straight body position. The hecht vault is rarely used because it also requires a great deal of upper body power and because the technique is often misunderstood by coaches. A member of the U.S.S.R. Olympic Team won the vaulting event in the 1960 Olympic Games with this vault.

Basic Description
(1-2) Jump with a rather low body position. This jumping posture provides an unusual amount of forward motion. Your body must be straight at the moment of contact with the horse; upper arms and upper body should form a nearly straight line. Your shoulders and chest move straight forward toward the horse in a horizontal path, and hands should contact the horse with arms stretched full length in front of you. This reach enables you to push downward toward hips for a longer period of time.
(3-4) Push downward forcefully. Keep head down and watch hands follow through as upper body passes over the horse. As a result of the push, upper body will bend slightly forward, creating a slight pike. Your legs should remain at approximately the same angle after the push.
(5) Raise upper body as knees pass over the horse, and tighten seat muscles to keep hips in a fixed position. Beginners tend to relax hips, arch too much, and raise head upward immediately after the push. Do not raise head; pass over the horse with a straight body.
(6-7) If your push and after-flight are strong, you should be able to land without piking down very much for the landing.

Prerequisites
Stoop vault. Lots of practice vaulting onto a trampoline (landing on your front) for distance. Extended push-ups on the floor.

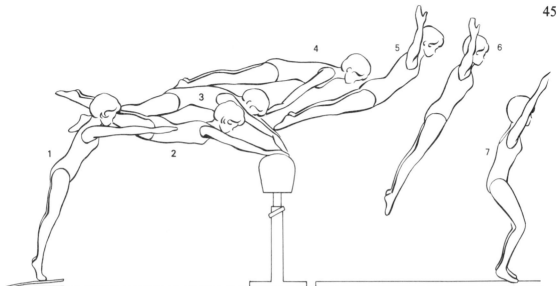

Hecht Vault

Spotting

Spot from the side by grasping upper body as arms move toward hips. Pull and raise performer over the horse. This is a difficult skill to hand-spot.

Round-off Backward One and a Half Somersault (Tucked Sukahara) Vault

Skill Level 9

This vault is often called a "Suk," which is short for Sukahara, the male Japanese gymnast who performed it for the first time in the 1972 Olympic Games in Munich, Germany. Eventually it was performed in a piked position, layout position, and with twists. The basic movement of the vault requires the gymnast to jump to the horse with a half twist to a short handstand position, with legs and hips behind the hands. This position, coupled with forward speed, sets the performer up for an aggressive piking action downward (snap-down). The two most important factors are the position before the snap-down and the snap-down itself.

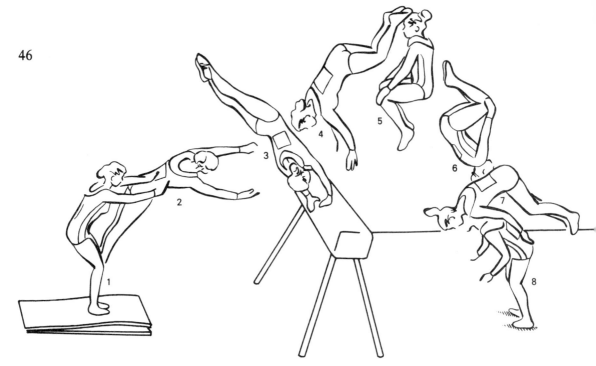

Round-off Backward One and a Half Somersault (Tucked Sukahara) Vault

Basic Description

(1-3) Execute a round-off with a low approach for a strong push off the horse. The arms are usually bent in preparation for a strong snap-down motion of the legs.

(4) Push with arms and extend shoulders for maximum snap-down.

(5-6) Pull knees into chest without throwing head backward. If head is thrown backward, it will retard your tucking and piking efforts.

(7-8) Open tuck and land with slightly bent knees.

Prerequisites

Experience executing a tucked backward somersault. Good snap-down from a handstand, with enough rotation to consistently land on your back on soft mats piled as high as the horse. Powerful round-off vault.

Spotting

The standard procedure in learning this skill is to pile soft mats as high as the horse on the far side of the horse. The gymnast then practices the round-off snap-down movement, landing on her back on the mats until she feels capable of additional rotation backward to her feet. After weeks (perhaps months) of demonstrating consistency in both phases of the vault, an excellent spotter must be used to insure backward somersault rotation during the actual vault. The mats are lowered by two feet and the spotter stands on the matted surface. As the round-off is completed, the spotter places a hand (the hand closest to the horse) on the performer's stomach, palm up. The other hand is then placed on performer's lower back as the snap-down occurs. The spotter then proceeds to somersault performer to her feet.

Spotting the Tucked Sukahara Vault

Forward Handspring to Forward One and a Half Somersault Vault

Skill Level 10

The power for this vault comes from the forward handspring. The basic problem for the gymnast is to achieve enough elevation off the vaulting board and enough rotation to continue rotating forward rapidly after the hand-push. This is accomplished by leaving the board with the hips in front of the feet (common to all vaults but particularly important here) to achieve unusually strong forward rotation. There is an obvious trade-off with respect to desired amount of rotation versus elevation. Another important factor is the placement of the board at an optimum distance from the horse to promote power. As a general rule, place the board as close as possible to promote function during the primary (somersault) phase of the vault.

As the gymnast pushes off the horse, she wants as much rotation speed with her feet as possible. If this speed is adequate, the next consideration is her quickness in assuming a tight tucked position for additional forward rotation

Forward Handspring to Forward One and a Half Somersault Vault

speed. To date, this vault has been performed in a piked position and with a half twist.

This vault may be practiced by piling soft mats on one side as high as the horse. The performer practices over-rotating a forward handspring to a front drop. As this technique improves, a spotter must be used to catch the completed version of the vault.

Basic Description

(1-7) Start with a strong run and pre-flight movement. Execute a handspring with powerful rotation. Your feet should pull you over the horse as hands make contact.

(8) Push with arms and extend shoulders.

(9-12) Bring upper body forward in a hunched, tucked position and grasp knees. Keeping knees apart at this point is not considered good form but it will aid rotation and allow you to see the landing better.

(13-15) Open the tuck and land with slightly bent knees.

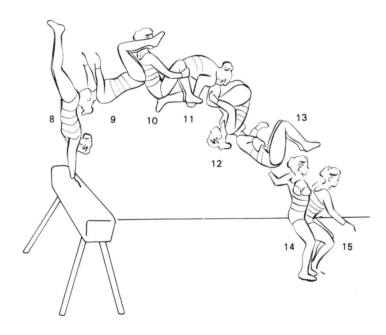

Prerequisites

Powerful handspring. Experience performing tucked front somersault.

Spotting

This skill is difficult to spot. Always use crash mats during practice. The spotter stands on two mats piled one atop the other on the far side of the horse. As performer completes the handspring, spotter places his or her near hand on performer's stomach, palm up. As performer ducks for the somersault, the other hand supports the back.

2

Balance Beam Brief History

The balance beam was one of the original hand-made pieces of apparatus developed for physical training by Frederick Jahn at the Hasenheide Turnplatz (exercise school) in Germany around 1811. The idea was probably based on "fence walking," still a common pastime of many youngsters. The first balance beams were similar to locker room benches, being wider and shorter than the modern variety. Early skill performances were limited to rolls combined with poses and simple dance movements. Eventually, the beam dimensions (longer and narrower) were standardized to accommodate longer dance sequences and to increase the difficulty of the balance factor. Today the balance beam is sixteen feet long, four inches wide, and about four feet off the floor. Its height can be lowered to create a low beam.

Movements on the Balance Beam

With the exception of mounts, dismounts, and a limited number of skills that require movement below the beam, a balance beam routine consists of *floor exercise* skills performed on a very re-

51

stricted, elevated surface. When executed on a narrow beam instead of a mat, these skills must be modified to allow for the fact that the feet, rather than held side by side, are usually positioned in a line that coincides with the axis of the beam. Modifications are also necessary because of restrictions on the length (limited distance) and width (increased difficulty in maintaining balance) of the performance area, and because of the risk involved in performing above the floor.

Like other gymnastic events, a balance beam routine begins with a mount and ends with a dismount. Mounts are usually confined to leaping, vaulting, or jumping to various handstands and rolls. The dismount may be any tumbling skill that ends in a landing with feet together, such as a handspring or somersault.

The bulk of a balance beam routine consists of dance elements, acrobatic and tumbling movements, and static poses. All components are linked together smoothly without superfluous motion. Included must be changes of pace and elevation, traveling (locomotor skills), leaving and returning to the beam, turns, and movements demonstrating flexibility and balance. All of these elements must be performed in a rhythmic, harmonious, artistic, and technically correct fashion.

Training on the Balance Beam

As with the other gymnastic events, the beginner is not expected to learn *all* of the skills described and illustrated here. Furthermore, it is impossible to present the skills strictly in order of increasing difficulty and, at the same time, introduce a wide variety of skill possibilities in their proper places in the book. Therefore, the reader must choose mounts, dismounts, and other skills that she can realistically expect to master given her particular ability level.

At first, learn a mount, dismount, and other skills that have a low difficulty rating. The walking and turning movements described are absolutely basic skills that every balance beam beginner must learn. Then, practice all of the half turns, some of the leaps and jumps, and the basic forward and backward rolls before selecting more difficult skills. As you proceed, you will begin to perceive the skill or skills that logically follow the one you are practicing. For instance, when you have learned the forward roll, you may wish to increase the difficulty of this skill by attempting one or more of its variations.

If you are a beginner, choose a relatively simple mount that will enable you to get on the beam with confidence and consistency. It is demoralizing to start your exercise by falling off or fighting to maintain your balance.

Consider how you will move out of the position in which you are left after the mount without having to include awkward or extra movements that are unrelated to your next skill. If additional movements must be included in this transition, be sure that they are well planned and pleasing to the eye.

Include skills in each of the categories mentioned above. Skills of the same category should be distributed throughout the routine. For instance, avoid grouping several different leaps together in one section of the exercise; instead, insert a leap at various intervals to add interest and variety.

Write down all of the skills that you can perform and list them under the name of the group to which they belong: mounts, leaps, turns, poses, hops, tumbling, and so on. On a sheet of paper, draw a long, narrow rectangle that represents a balance beam. Find a quiet retreat where you can think and perform some simple movements. Measure off a section of floor space about the length of a balance beam and start planning a routine. This procedure will enable you to plot your routine on paper as you measure and perform most of the skills in the allotted space.

Following is an outline of a basic balance beam routine.

(1) *Mount* with a skill you have mastered.
(2) *Dance*
   - *Leaps:* Perform at least two.
   - *Poses:* The number of *momentary* stops allowed is unlimited. Longer holds are restricted to three.
   - *Turns and Pirouettes:* Four or five are recommended. A 360-degree (or more) pirouette should be executed in an advanced routine.
   - *Low Movement: See* "Floor Exercise Composition" in *Women's Gymnastics 1.*
   - *Modern Dance: See* "Dance and the Floor Exercise Event" in *Women's Gymnastics 1.*
(3) *Tumbling and Acrobatics*
   - Three skills for beginners and at least five for more advanced performers.
(4) *Dismount* with a skill that is more difficult and spectacular than those of the rest of the routine.

Remember, execute all movements confidently and rhythmically, include changes of pace and elevation, and perform an interesting variety of skills. This event is *timed,* so find out and observe the specified time limit.

BALANCE BEAM SKILLS

It is hard to separate the balance beam event from the floor exercise event. Except for mounts and dismounts, almost all of the skills in these events are similar, the major difference being a narrow beam surface that dictates slower movements and a greater emphasis on balance than in the floor exercise event. It is strongly recommended that you study these balance beam skills in conjunction with *Women's Gymnastics 1,* which teaches the primary gymnastic and dance skills of the floor exercise event.

Lack of space requires confining the following instructions and illustrations to selected skills that are particularly common in the balance beam event.

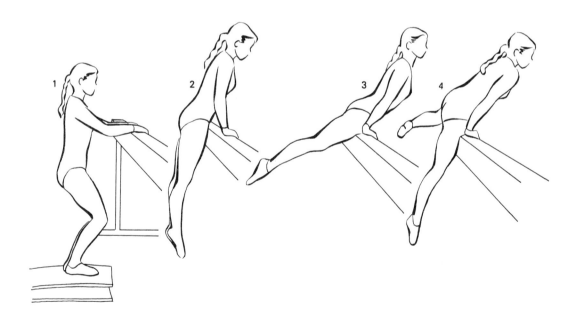

Front Support Quarter Turn to Straddle Mount

Front Support Quarter Turn to Straddle Mount

Skill Level 1

Swing your leg forward and turn with an even rhythm that demonstrates good form and control.

Basic Description

(1-4) Stand on the side of the beam and facing it. Place hands on top of the beam. Jump to a front support and swing one leg over the beam to begin the quarter turn.

(5-7) Complete the quarter turn, so that you are facing the length of the beam. Move forward hand next to other hand.

Spotting

Hold performer's hips during turn.

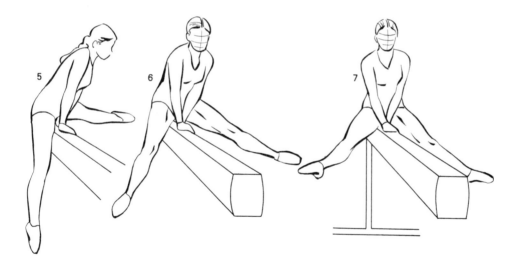

Single-Leg Squat Mount

Skill Level 1

When this mount is completed, your shoulders must lean forward in front of your hands to counterbalance the weight of your extended rear leg.

Basic Description

(1-3) Jump and squat on one leg, with leg between your arms on the beam. The other leg may be extended to the side or to the rear.

Spotting

Stand on either side of performer and grasp her upper arm to stabilize her.

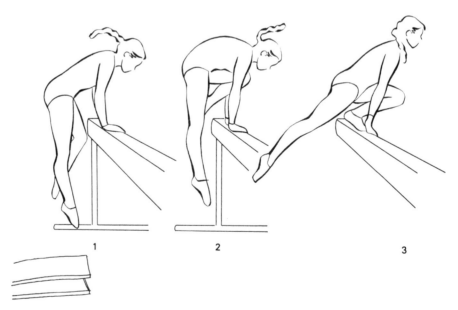

1   2   3

Single-Leg Squat Mount

Squat Mount

Skill Level 1

After you jump, use your arms for control as you execute the squat stand.

Basic Description

(1–3) Jump and squat on both legs, with legs between your arms on the beam in a squat stand.

Spotting

Same as for the single-leg squat mount.

1   2   3

Squat Mount

Straddle Mount

Skill Level 1

Your shoulders must be held forward in front of your hands to compensate for the weight of your hips in the rear.

Basic Description
(1-3) Jump and straddle legs outside of arms in a straddle stand.

Spotting
Spot from in front by grasping performer's upper arms as the jump occurs.

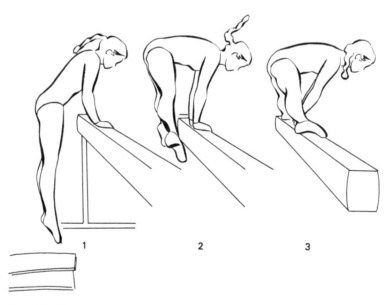

Straddle Mount

Squat to Rear Support Mount

Skill Level 3

Pass through the squat very quickly because it is difficult to hold a tight squat position for even a moment.

Basic Description

(1-3) After a short, premeasured run, jump, grasp the beam, and quickly bring legs between your hands. Raise hips as little as possible as legs pass over the beam. Keep shoulders over the beam for balance.

  (4) Quickly extend legs and hips to a rear support position. As extension occurs, lean shoulders backward to compensate for the weight of extended legs.

Spotting

Stand on the far side of the beam. Grasp performer's upper arms, from the side, and stabilize her as she comes over the beam.

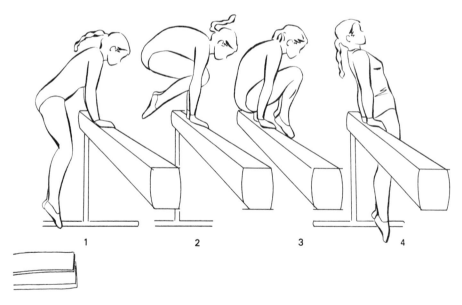

1   2   3   4

Squat to Rear Support Mount

Stride Jump to Rear Support Mount (Variation)

Skill Level 4

Practice this skill on a broad, elevated surface before attempting it on the beam. Notice that the shoulders are always slightly behind the hands during the squat. Spot this skill from the rear and control the support position.

Stride Jump to Rear Support Mount

Straddle "L" Mount

Skill Level 5

Practice holding this position on the floor before attempting it on the beam. Your legs should be held parallel with the floor.

Basic Description

(1-4) Jump and raise hips with legs straddled.

    (5) Balance on your arms as you bring legs forward to straddle "L" position.

Spotting

Spot from the front by holding performer's upper arms to aid balance.

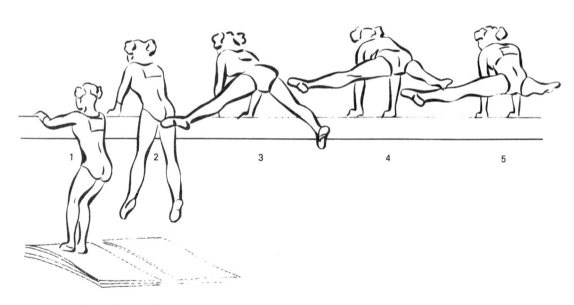

Straddle "L" Mount

Side Step-on Mount

Skill Level 2

Premeasure your steps for the approach and push off with the same foot every time. Your body weight shifts from your support hand to your right foot as your left leg moves forward.

Basic Description

(1) Place vaulting board almost parallel with the beam. Take a couple of premeasured running steps along the side of the beam.

(2-3) Step onto board with one foot. Place opposite hand on top of the beam next to your hip. Kick leg closest to the beam (rear leg) upward above the beam.

(4) Press down with support arm and move shoulder over the beam. Bring kicking leg down on the beam.

(5-6) Balance on one leg with bent knee and arm support as other leg is brought up and extended forward.

Spotting

Grasp upper arm from far side of beam and stabilize performer.

Side Step-on Mount

Side Step-on to Squat Mount (Variation)

Skill Level 2

This variation puts you in position for a squat turn, roll, or stand. Your body weight shifts from your support arm to your left foot and right foot in succession. The spotter stands on the far side and guides the support arm.

Side Step-on Half Turn Mount (Variation)

Skill Level 2

Maintain some weight on your right arm until the turn is completed. This turning movement during the mount adds an element of surprise. The spotter should stand to the rear of the performer and guide the support arm during the jump and turn.

Side Step-on to Squat Mount

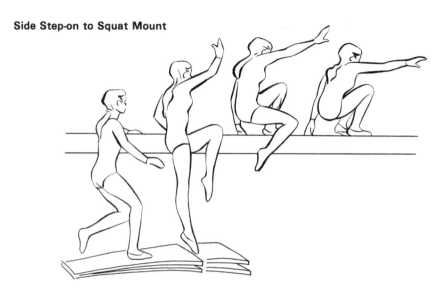

Side Step-on Half Turn Mount

Hitch Kick Mount

Skill Level 2

The left support arm must constantly guide your body and support its weight until the sit occurs.

Basic Description

  (1) *See* side step-on mount.
(2-4) Step onto board with right foot, grasp beam with left hand, and kick rear leg forward and completely over the beam. Keep kick low so that you skim over the beam.
(5-8) Quickly bring right leg over the beam just before the sit. Bend right knee and hold the beam with right hand to stabilize sitting position.

Spotting

Stabilize performer's hips from the rear during the jump.

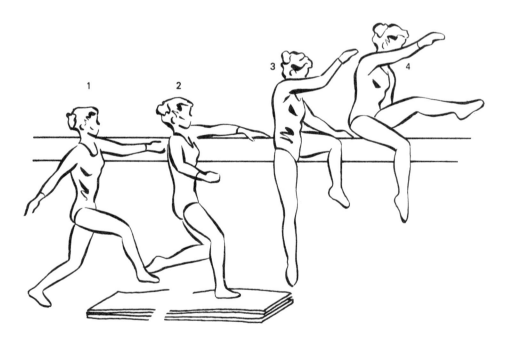

Hitch Kick Mount

Step-up Mount

Skill Level 3

It is advisable to begin practicing this mount by leaping onto a broad surface about the same height as the beam. Thereafter, leap to lower beam levels until you can mount from the floor with the beam at regulation height.

Place the vaulting board one long step away from the beam to give your jump distance as well as elevation.

Basic Description
(1-2) Run toward the end of the beam with premeasured steps.
(3-7) Step onto the board with one foot, swing rear leg forward, and leap to a stand on the end of the beam. Establish balance on support leg before bringing rear leg forward.

Spotting
The spotter may grasp performer's hand and run alongside her. As the leap occurs, spotter's arm is kept rigid to provide support.

Step-up Mount

1   2   3   4   5   6   7

Forward Roll Mount

Skill Level 4

Learn this skill on a beam with a padded surface to protect your head and upper back during the roll. Be sure to use a spotter.

Basic Description

(1-4) Stand or run and jump to a momentary free front piked support position on the end or side of the beam. As hands contact beam, bend elbows and move hips over head. Your arms must guide your body throughout. Watch the beam until your head almost touches.

(5-6) Tuck head, roll onto your upper back, and quickly shift hands to an under-beam grasp. Pull with arms to lower your body onto the beam with control.

You may also perform the forward roll mount with a continuation of the roll, rotating to your feet and then standing up. In this case, the hands do not shift to the bottom of the beam.

Prerequisites

Experience with forward rolls on the floor and beam.

Spotting

Stand on a broad surface (mats or a spotting platform) near the end and to the side of the beam. Grasp performer's hips with both hands, lift, and guide the roll throughout.

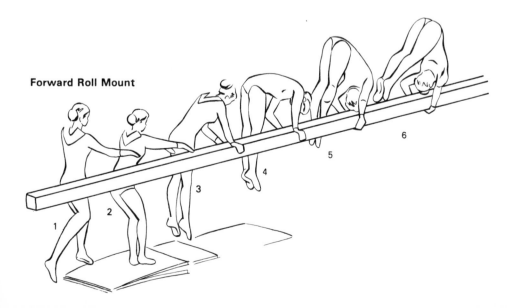

Forward Roll Mount

Jump to Handstand Mount

Skill Level 8

Learn this mount from the side of the beam before attempting it on the end. The side handstand is somewhat easier because the hands may be placed much farther apart. The leg positions may vary once the handstand position has been achieved.

Basic Description

(1-2) Stand or run and jump. Place hands on the beam after the jump or place them on the beam while standing.

(3-5) Pike with a lower back arch and straddle legs as wide as possible. Your arms will be bent at the beginning of the jump but should be straightened as hips move over your head.

Jump to Handstand Mount

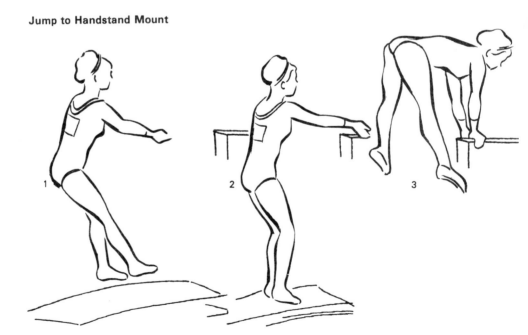

(6-7) Your shoulders will move slightly in front of hands until hips are above your head. The shoulders are then gently pressed back over hands as you establish a balanced position.

Prerequisites

A well-controlled handstand. Straight-arm bent-hip straddle press to a handstand. Ability to turn out of the handstand if an overbalance occurs.

Spotting

Stand on a spotting platform or on the floor if a low beam is used to practice this skill. Grasp hips and guide performer throughout.

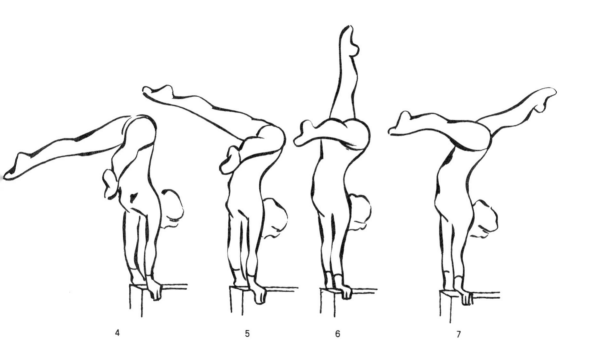

4   5   6   7

Straight-Arm-and-Leg Press to Handstand Mount (Variation)

Skill Level 9

The straight-arm press to a handstand requires strength, flexibility, and balance. Unlike the usual procedure in executing a handstand, in the press to a handstand the legs and upper body are brought up *slowly* to the vertical position. The prerequisites are the ability to hold a handstand and a fairly wide straddle position. The illustration demonstrates one of the most difficult straight-arm presses used in women's gymnastics, one that starts from a straddle "L" position with the body in a near-sitting position.

Several methods may be employed when learning the straight-arm press. One, of course, is to try the press itself as often as possible. Another is to perform a handstand against a wall and then reverse the movement, slowly lowering until you are standing on the floor. This technique strengthens the same muscles used in pressing to a handstand. Perform this drill five or six times at the end of every workout.

In another method of training for this press, the gymnast stands on the edge of mats piled one atop the other, placing her substantially above the floor. She puts her hands on the floor and attempts the press with her hips halfway up to the handstand position at the start. The mats are gradually lowered as she learns to press from lower and lower levels.

Straight-Arm-and-Leg Press to Handstand Mount

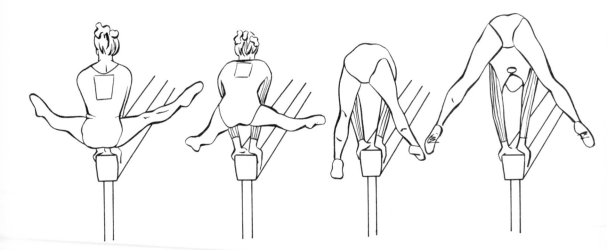

Another procedure requires a spotter, who assists the performer by lifting her hips over her head as she begins the press.

These methods have worked for many gymnasts; however, there are some very good gymnasts who have difficulty with this skill. In any case, practice the press to a handstand on the floor before attempting it on the balance beam. Like the jump to a handstand mount, this skill is considerably easier when executed from the side of the beam.

Basic Description
(1) Stand with feet slightly apart. Place hands on the floor about shoulder width apart.
(2) Lean forward slightly and shift your weight to your arms. Push downward on the floor and round your back. Continue leaning and pressing as feet leave the floor, and straddle legs as wide as possible. Your hips should elevate and move over your head as you arch your lower back.
(3) Once you have achieved a balanced position with hips over your head, slowly raise legs and bring them together.
(4) As you assume the handstand position, tuck hips under (aligned vertically with the rest of your body) and tighten seat muscles to avoid overarching.

Here is how the straight-arm-and-leg press to a handstand mount looks on the balance beam.

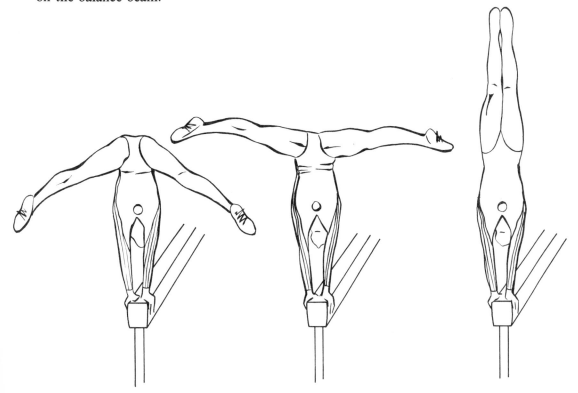

Aerial Walkover Mount

Skill Level 6

For a more difficult version of this mount, place your hands on the beam after your seat touches.

Basic Description

(1-3) Premeasure your steps up to the board carefully. Execute a skip step (step forward, hop, then step forward with other foot) and bend over just in front of the beam for the walkover. Move arms out to the sides and to the rear.

Aerial Walkover Mount

(4-6) Kick as you reach backward past your hips and place hands on the beam. Watch the floor as your seat contacts the beam. Do not attempt to execute a high walkover. Your seat should just meet the beam and your upper body should fall smoothly into position.

(7-9) Join legs and pull upper body forward into a rear support position.

Prerequisite
Aerial walkover in the floor exercise event.

Spotting
Stand on the side. Grasp and support performer's lower back as she bends down and kicks over. Stabilize the rear support position.

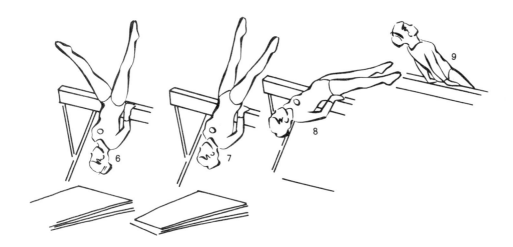

WALKING THE BEAM

Walking Forward

Skill Level 1

Practice walking on a low beam before proceeding to the high beam. Your posture should be a prime consideration when walking. Walk with hips tucked under and upper body held very erect. Keep your head in line with upper body and watch the beam; never watch your feet as you move. Your arms may be held out to the sides while practicing. With each step, hold leg turned out from the hip, bring rear foot forward along the side of the beam, and point your toe. Your steps should be short and gliding, your weight on the balls of your feet. Try walking with a high kick before each step, and practice running with short, fast steps.

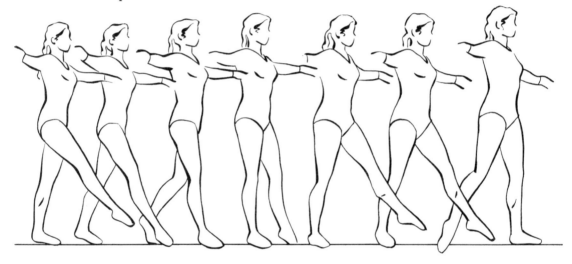

Walking Forward

Walking Backward

Skill Level 1

Walking backward will teach you to think ahead, and will give you a strong sense of the restrictions imposed by a four-inch surface. Follow the instructions for walking forward. Be careful not to step off the beam.

Walking Backward

Walking Sideways

Skill Level 1

Step-together-step with a smooth sliding or hopping action will help teach you the importance of good body alignment.

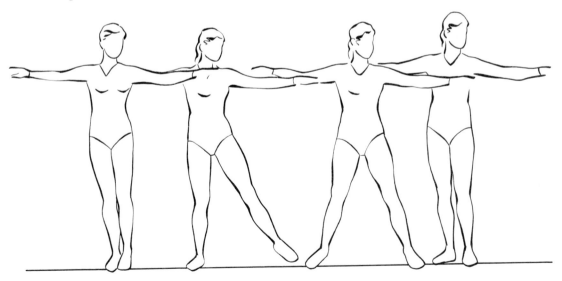

Walking Sideways

Walking with Changes of Elevation and Pace

Skill Level 1

Practice walking both flat-footed and high on the balls of your feet for changes of foot (ankle) elevation. Walk with bent knees and with alternately bent and extended knees. Combine slow and fast walking until you can perform a smooth run along the beam.

HOPS, LEAPS, AND JUMPS

Skipping

Skill Level 1

Practice skip steps—step-hop-step—on the beam until you are comfortable and consistent. Attempt to skip long and low as well as high and short.

Skipping

Bent-Knees Hop

Skill Level 4

Step forward on left foot and lift right leg forward-upward, with slightly bent knee, as you push off with left foot. Assume the position illustrated and land on left foot. Various leg positions may be used when performing this hop (and all other leaps and hops) if the positions are pleasing.

Bent-Knees Hop

Chassé

Skill Level 1

Step-close-step with a push off forward foot. The forward leg always remains in front. Perform this skill in a series across the beam.

Chassé

Leap to Squat Position

Skill Level 1

Take one or two walking steps and kick rear leg forward as you push off the beam with other leg. End the landing in a low squat position.

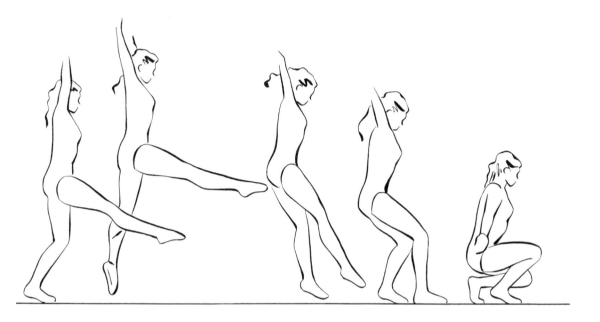

Leap to Squat Position

Leap to Single-Leg Squat Position

Skill Level 2

Take one or two walking steps and kick rear leg forward as you push off the beam with other leg. Land on forward foot, with other leg held rearward. Bring rear leg forward and squat as illustrated. Other leaps may be substituted prior to the single-leg squat.

Split Leap

Skill Level 4

Step forward on right foot and push off while lifting left knee. Split legs as much as possible and land on left foot.

Split Leap

Leap to Single-Leg Squat Position

Switch Split Hop (Variation)

Skill Level 5

Step forward on right foot and push off while kicking left leg forward. Quickly switch legs and split as much as possible before landing on right foot.

Switch Split Hop

Squat Jump

Skill Level 2

Practice jumping from a stand to a squat or from a squat to a stand. You may also jump from a squat back to a squat position.

Squat Jump

Sissone

Skill Level 2

Step forward with left foot. Bring right foot forward to the rear of left foot and jump. Land on left foot. This skill may be performed with a landing on either foot.

Sissone

Split Jump

Skill Level 4

Jump from both feet and split legs as much as possible before landing.

Split Jump

Stretched Turn on Both Feet

Skill Level 1

Stand on the balls of your feet with one foot slightly ahead of the other. Rise on the balls of your feet as you turn in the direction that corresponds to rear foot. Initiate the turn by pulling one shoulder (rear foot side) and pivoting on both feet in the direction of the turn. You may step into this turn, bringing rear foot in front of other foot for the turn as illustrated, or start from a stand or squat stand.

Stretched Turn on Both Feet

Stretched Turn on One Foot

Skill Level 1

Step forward on left foot as you push with right foot into a right turn on left foot. Your right leg moves sideways and rearward as you turn. This turn may also be performed in the other direction and/or with free leg held in various positions.

Squat Turn

Skill Level 1

From a stretch stand, with right toe held a couple of inches behind left heel, squat and turn to the right. Always try to turn with a smooth, flowing motion.

Squat Turn

Stretched Turn on One Foot

Forward Kick Turn

Skill Level 1

Basic Description

(1-3)   Step forward on right foot. Kick left leg forward.

(4-7)   At the peak of the kick, pivot on right foot and turn hips and upper body a half turn to the right. Hold left leg to the rear as high as possible without bending upper body forward. Keep hip muscles tight for stability. If you wish to modify the final position, you may hold left leg high to the rear with a bent knee.

Forward Kick Turn

Backward Kick Turn (Variation)

Skill Level 1

The final position in this turn may be modified by bending the extended leg and/or using other arm positions.

Backward Kick Turn

Outward Pirouette with Bent Knee

Skill Level 3

Basic Description

(1-3) Step forward with left foot. Turn head and shoulders right as you bend right knee.

(4-6) Swing right leg right in a circular pattern as you pivot on left foot. The right leg is extended forward in the final position. Keeping hip muscles tight will help you maintain balance when performing this and other full pirouettes. Any bend in the waist will probably result in a miss.

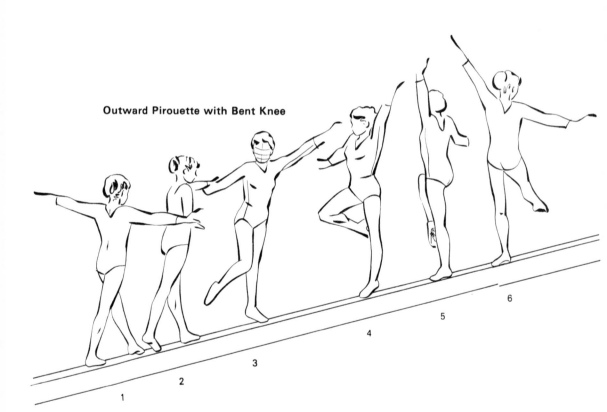

Outward Pirouette with Bent Knee

Inward Half Pirouette with Bent Knee

Skill Level 3

Basic Description
(1) Step forward with left foot and turn shoulders slightly to the right with arms extended to the sides (arm position optional).
(2) Swing arms and shoulders to the left and begin raising right leg.
(3-5) Continue swinging upper body to the left in a circular pattern, and execute a half turn with right leg held in the illustrated position.

Inward Half Pirouette with Bent Knee

Simple turns can be made more elaborate by changing arm and leg positions. Variations of this turn include: holding the high leg to the rear throughout; bending the high leg and extending it for the finish; swinging your high leg forward after the turn and executing another turn; executing more than a half turn.

Inward Full Pirouette (Variation)

Skill Level 5

Do not hesitate during this or any other pirouette. The movement should be smooth and continuous for proper execution and to maintain balance.

Inward Full Pirouette

Lunge to Inward One and a Half Pirouette

Skill Level 7

Lunge turns provide a pleasing change of elevation in a routine. You may execute any number of turns in this position.

Basic Description

(1) Take a big step forward with left foot and bend left knee (deep lunge position). Hold left arm in front of chest and extend right arm to the rear. This arm position makes upper body turn slightly to the right.

(2) Swing arms and shoulders in a circular pattern to the left.

(3-11) Swing right leg outward and forward in a circular pattern, and continue rotating leg and upper body as you pivot on left foot through one and a half turns.

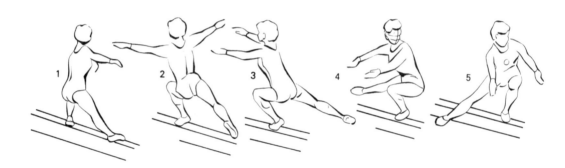

Lunge to Inward One and a Half Pirouette

When practicing this skill, you may work your way up to one and a half turns in stages, stopping after a half turn or after a full turn by placing your right foot on the beam.

Note that the performer in the illustration has chosen to rise to a stand during the final half turn.

You may also execute an *outward* lunge pirouette by turning in the direction that corresponds to the outstretched leg.

Refer to the routines section at the end of this chapter for additional turns and pirouettes.

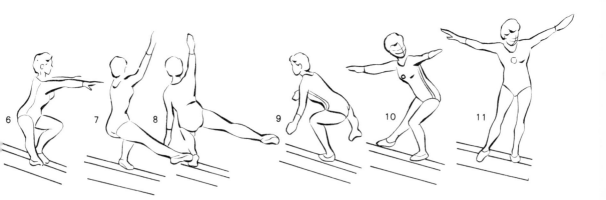

HOLD POSITIONS (POSES)

The usual purpose of hold positions is to demonstrate exceptional balance and/or flexibility. However, positions that do not demonstrate these qualities may be held for an instant (less than one second) as a means of recovery from a shaky movement that would otherwise place the performer in an awkward position; as a rest position that allows the performer to compose herself before

moving into her next skill; as a pose with a graceful "body line" that is pleasant to look at; or as a position that helps to develop the "character" (style) of an exercise. Pose positions should be interspersed throughout an exercise. Although there are no hard and fast rules, five to ten poses in a single routine is about average. Remember, these are often only momentary pauses rather than one-second holds requiring great flexibility or balancing skill.

TUMBLING AND ACROBATICS

Any tumbling or acrobatic skill that can be performed on the floor can also be performed on the balance beam; aside from the special restrictions that the balance beam imposes on the gymnast's placement of her hands and feet, the techniques are analogous in both events. Therefore, as mentioned earlier, it would be useful to study the "Tumbling and Acrobatics" chapter of *Women's Gymnastics 1* before beginning work on the following skills.

Backward Shoulder Roll

Skill Level 1

This skill is quite similar to a backward shoulder roll on the floor. The performer should try several of these rolls before executing her first shoulder roll on the beam. Placement of the head on the side of the beam allows the beginning performer to roll over more efficiently.

Backward Shoulder Roll

Basic Description

(1-3) Lie on your back with your head held to the left side of the beam. Place left hand on the beam (heel of hand on top, fingers down the side of the beam) next to face. Place right hand on the bottom of the beam for pulling power and stability. Raise legs from the beam to begin the roll.

(4) Bring legs and hips over right shoulder.

(5) Separate legs and place right knee on the beam as close to right shoulder as possible. Shift right hand from the bottom to the top of the beam as your weight is transferred to right knee.

(6) Push with your arms and raise upper body with left leg held high in the rear or in position for your next skill.

Prerequisite

Backward shoulder roll on the floor.

Spotting

Spot by holding and stabilizing the hips, from the rear, as the roll occurs.

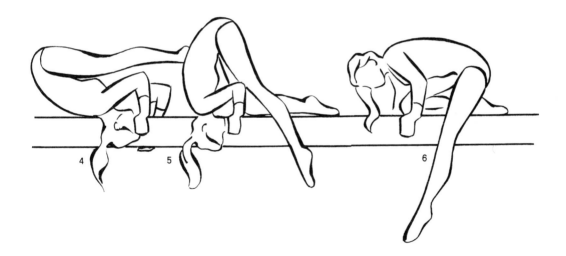

Backward Roll

Skill Level 2

Beginners will find it difficult to push with their arms after the first toe touches the beam. Roll backward in an uninterrupted movement so that your hips move over your head efficiently.

Basic Description

 (1) Lie on your back with hands on the beam under shoulders. Your thumbs and heels of your hands rest on the top of the beam and your fingers extend down the sides. Raise legs to begin the roll.

(2-4) Bring legs and hips over your head. Your arms keep pressure off your head during the roll. Bend knees, push with arms, and place the balls of your feet on the beam. Your legs may be separated during the roll for a knee scale (knee and lower leg on the beam, other leg extended to the rear), or your toes may be hooked as they touch the beam as in the illustration.

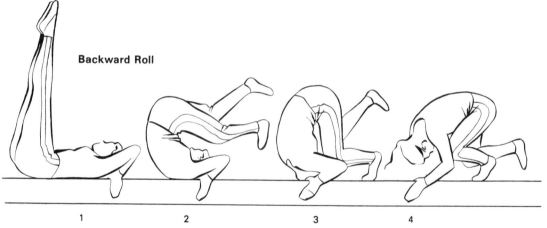

Backward Roll

1   2   3   4

Prerequisite

Backward roll on the floor.

Spotting

Spot by guiding performer's hips from the rear during the roll. Assist performer's arm push by lifting hips as her head touches the beam.

Forward Roll

Skill Level 2

Practice this skill on a padded beam if possible because excessive repetition often bruises the cervical projections of the spine.

Basic Description

(1-3) Stand with one foot slightly behind the other. Lower to a squat position, bend forward, and place hands on the beam (fingers down the sides with thumb and heel of thumb on top). Watch the beam as long as possible before ducking your head for the roll.

(4-5) Carefully bend arms and lower the back of your head (between arms) and your back to the beam.

(6-7) As you transfer your weight from your arms to your back, quickly shift hands to grip the bottom of the beam (move elbows close to your head) and pull to stabilize the roll. Release your grips and continue into your next movement.

Forward Roll

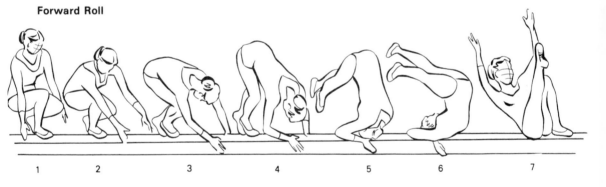

1   2   3   4   5   6   7

Prerequisite
Forward roll on the floor.

Spotting
Spot by guiding performer's hips throughout the roll.

Pike into Forward Roll (Variation)

Skill Level 3

Flexibility of knee and ankle joints is important in this forward rolling technique.

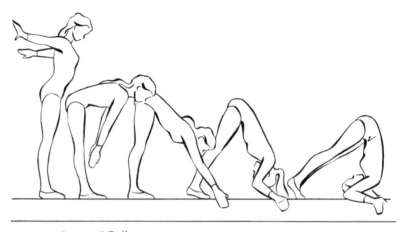

Pike into Forward Roll

Forward Roll from Knees (Variation)

Skill Level 2

Push with toes until legs straighten. Shift hands to grip the bottom of the beam as shoulders bear weight.

Forward Roll from Knees

Arabesque into Forward Roll (Variation)

Skill Level 2

This skill requires a great deal of leg flexibility. Keep your toe in touch with the beam as long as possible and do not allow your hips to drop as you roll.

Arabesque into Forward Roll

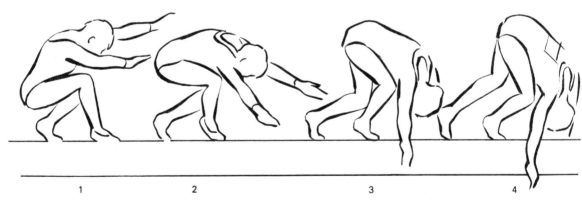

| 1 | 2 | 3 | 4 |

Forward Roll Without Hands

Forward Roll Without Hands

Skill Level 5

Practice this roll on a soft surface at first. This roll must be executed rather fast to minimize the possibility of rolling sideways.

Basic Description

(1-2)   Step forward and bend front knee. Lower upper body over front leg and hold arms out to the sides. Bring head as close as possible to the beam while maintaining balance. Align your body with the beam by watching the beam continuously until you duck your head.

(3-8)   Duck your head and place the back of your head and upper back on the beam with a smooth rolling action. Roll forward to a bent-knee sit, straddle, or other position.

Prerequisites

Forward roll on the beam. Forward roll on the floor without hands.

Spotting

Spot from the front and catch performer's hips as roll occurs.

5   6   7   8

Arabesque to Forward Roll Without Hands (Variation)

Skill Level 6

The head touches the beam as the push occurs and the roll moves quickly to a squat stand.

Arabesque to Forward Roll Without Hands

Handstand Forward Roll

Skill Level 5

Basic Description

(1) Kick to a controlled handstand. Overbalance *slightly;* if you overbalance too much, your hips will drop too fast as you lower into the piked position.

(2-4) Bend elbows and pike with a smooth motion. Watch the beam until your head is nearly touching it. Place the back of your head and upper back on the beam as legs move downward toward your face. (The piking action on contact lessens the shock.) As weight is transferred from your arms to your back, quickly shift hands to an under-the-beam pulling position.

Prerequisites

Controlled handstand on the floor. Forward roll on the beam.

Spotting

Both the handstand and the roll must be spotted. Adjust the beam to a low position or pile up mats for greater spotting elevation. Hold performer from the side by grasping her legs. Guide and support performer throughout the descent into the roll.

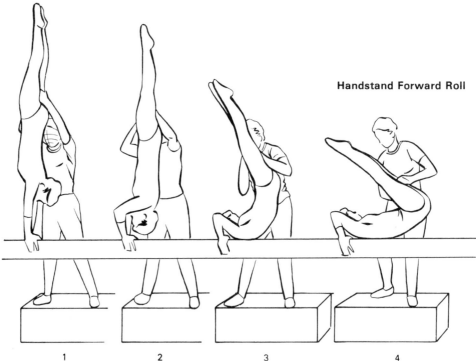

Handstand Forward Roll

| 1 | 2 | 3 | 4 |

Cartwheel

Skill Level 4

Practicing on a low beam is essential because placing the feet on the beam as you land is difficult.

Basic Description

(1) Stand facing the length of the beam. Step forward about twenty-four inches with right foot.

(2-3) Bend right knee forty-five degrees and lean forward so that your stomach is fairly close to your thigh. Place right hand on the beam (fingers down side of beam) as you kick rear leg over your head and rotate your body a quarter turn. Be sure leading leg moves directly over your head or you will be off-balance sideways as you land. Place left hand on the beam immediately after right hand goes down; hands should be about shoulder width apart. Keep eyes on the beam between hands and split legs as much as possible.

(4-5) Rotate another quarter turn as you bring left foot down on the beam about six inches from left hand. Extend shoulders and transfer weight from arms to left leg. Stand on both feet facing the length of the beam as illustrated, or with right leg held high in the rear.

1   2   3   4   5

Cartwheel

Prerequisites

Cartwheel along a line on the floor. Practice cartwheeling out of a still handstand.

Spotting

Spot from the rear and guide performer's hips throughout.

Variations of the cartwheel include the one-arm cartwheel with either arm and modifications of the starting and finishing positions.

Far-Arm One-Arm Cartwheel (Variation)

Skill Level 5

One-arm cartwheels require the performer to keep the support shoulder over the support hand as she passes through the handstand position.

Far-Arm One-Arm Cartwheel

Backward Pirouette Step-out

Skill Level 6

Learn this skill on the floor and the low beam. The initial kick should be soft so that a near-handstand position can be achieved prior to the step-out.

Backward Pirouette Step-out

Backward Walkover

Backward Walkover

Skill Level 6

Practice this skill along a floor line and graduate to a low beam before attempting a high beam walkover. Be sure that you are aligned with the line or beam before you commit yourself for the backward arch. Once you start, it is difficult to stop.

Basic Description
    (1) Stand with arms overhead and weight on rear leg. The forward leg may be raised or placed slightly in front of support foot. Stretch upward through your stomach.

(2-3) Arch backward with weight on support leg.

    (4) Place hands on the beam as close to support leg as possible. Try to see support leg as hands touch the beam.

(5-8) Push off slightly bent support leg and kick forward leg over your head. Split legs as much as possible and do not let shoulders sag forward as your body passes through handstand. Push out in shoulders.

    (9) Place leading leg on the beam close to hands and stand with other leg held as high as possible.

Prerequisites
Backward walkover on the floor with excellent body positions and control. Considerable control in a handstand position on the beam.

Spotting
The performer should be spotted on all walkovers until the recovery phase is executed consistently. Spot from the side by supporting lower back and assisting kicking leg.

Valdez (Variation)

Skill Level 6

Keep your support shoulder over your support hand until the handstand position is reached. Sustain the push with your support foot as long as possible.

Valdez

Forward Walkover

Skill Level 6

If you are flexible enough, you will be able to see your first foot as it touches the beam for the stand.

Basic Description

(1-2) Stand with arms extended overhead. Raise one leg and step forward.

(3-4) Bend forward knee slightly and place hands on the beam about twelve inches in front of foot. Raise extended rear leg.

(5-6) Kick through a handstand position and keep head up so that the beam can be observed as long as possible. Split legs as much as you can.

(7) Stretch upward in shoulders as you place first foot on the beam as close to hands as possible. Do not allow shoulders to sag forward.

(8-9) Shift body weight from hands to first foot. Keep head back and arch your back as much as possible as you stand.

Forward Walkover

Prerequisites

Forward walkover on the floor with excellent body position and control. Considerable control in a handstand.

Spotting

Spot performer's lower back throughout.

Spotting the Forward Walkover

Aerial Walkover

Skill Level 9

This skill is very difficult because it requires a great deal of precision. Missing the beam with the first foot upon landing is one of the most serious mistakes that can be made.

First learn to perform the aerial walkover on a floor line. Proceed to a low beam with side platform extensions that broaden the landing surface.

Most performers will have to place their landing foot farther under their hip than the performer in the illustration does. Her powerful kick provides her with enough rotation and elevation to bring her foot down slightly in front of her hip.

Basic Description

(1-2) Step forward with arms overhead. Bend both legs slightly as you lean forward with a smooth motion. Your arms follow your upper body as you bend.

(3-5) Quickly kick rear leg overhead as you lift arms side-rearward. Keep your eyes on the beam and split legs as much as possible.

(6-8) Strain to place landing foot under your hip; this will help insure a secure landing position. Continue leading with hip (arching) as you bring upper body up to a stand.

Aerial Walkover

Prerequisite
Excellent aerial walkover on the floor that demonstrates exceptional flexibility.

Spotting
Spot by supporting lower back and hips, and by stabilizing the gymnast during the landing.

6

7

8

Aerial Cartwheel (Variation)

Skill Level 9

Practice aerial cartwheels on a floor line before attempting them on a low beam. Watch the beam throughout. As with all aerial skills, practice will develop consistency and confidence.

Aerial Cartwheel

Backward Handspring

Skill Level 7

The beam backward handspring is usually a somewhat modified version of this skill. The hands may be staggered slightly when brought down on the beam to provide more surface support. The last phase (snap-down) is usually "toned down" for better control in the landing unless an aggressive dismount is to follow.

Basic Description

(1-4) Thrust hips slightly farther forward and cover less distance after the push with the legs than in the backward handspring on the floor. The upper body whips around very fast.

(5-7) Unlike the method employed in a tumbling handspring, there is usually very little push with the arms during the second phase for a slower, more controlled movement that provides greater stability. As your execution of this skill improves, you may try performing it in the more aggressive manner of the floor backward handspring.

Backward Handspring

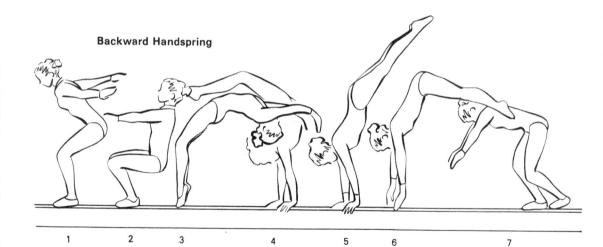

1   2   3   4   5   6   7

Prerequisites

Backward handspring on the floor. Backward walkover on the beam.

Spotting

Spot with both hands on performer's hips during the initial stages of learning. A spotting belt may be used, with two spotters, to provide freedom of movement. The spotter must elevate and support hips enough to allow performer to place her hands on the beam properly.

Backward Handspring Step-out (Variation)

Skill Level 7

Splitting your legs as you pass through the handstand position and stepping out softens the landing and makes it safer.

Backward Handspring Step-out

One-Arm Backward Handspring (Variation)

Skill Level 8

Do not let your shoulder sag or your arm buckle as your hand touches the beam. Be sure you can execute this skill on a floor line before attempting it on a low beam.

Two types of backward somersaults are commonly done on the beam: the aerial backward walkover to a step-out and the tucked backward somersault to a two-foot landing.

Aerial Backward Walkover

Skill Level 8

This is a fast, low, whippy skill rather than an elevated somersault. The lead, step-out foot is brought around very aggressively to place it under the hip in time for the landing. Use a beam with side platform extensions while learning this skill.

Aerial Backward Walkover

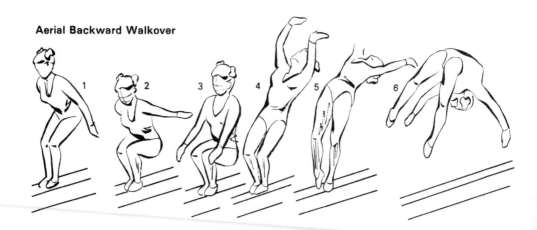

Basic Description

(1-2) Stand with arms overhead. Simultaneously bend knees ninety degrees and swing arms in a semicircle with a smooth motion until they are well behind hips.

(3-5) Throw arms forward-upward as you push off with legs. This action is very similar to a backward handspring throw except that you do not lean as far backward.

(6) Continue throwing arms, head, and chest around and under hips. Separate legs and move arms out to the sides as feet leave the beam.

(7-8) Split legs as much as possible and reach for the beam with lead foot.

(9-10) Hold head low and watch the beam as you land. Bend leg slightly to absorb the shock as the step-out occurs. Step backward onto other leg with control.

Prerequisites

Aerial backward walkover on the floor. Backward walkover on the beam. Backward handspring on the beam.

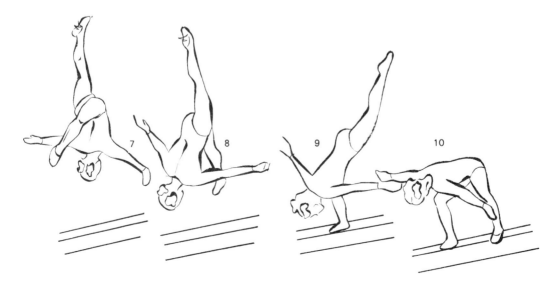

Spotting

Spot this skill as a backward handspring is spotted, except that hips must be given additional assistance to aid in elevation. A spotting belt provides very effective support for this skill.

Tucked Backward Somersault (Variation)

Skill Level 9

Except for a slightly staggered foot position, the tucked backward somersault is performed on the beam as it is on the floor. Most performers land with their upper bodies held rather low to insure stability in the landing.

Tucked Backward Somersault

DISMOUNTS

Balance beam dismounts fall into two basic categories: hand support dismounts and somersault dismounts. Most of these are executed from the side of the beam or off the end. It is often desirable to land close to your point of departure on the beam since elevation is usually more important than distance. As with all tumbling and dismount skills in other events, the performer should have enough rotation power to be able to assume an extended body position prior to landing and thus land in a fairly erect standing position. All landings should be executed with slightly bent knees and hips to absorb the shock on impact.

The performer's head should be aligned with her upper body but she must watch the mat as the landing occurs.

Kick to Front Vault Dismount

Skill Level 1

This dismount may be performed from a single-leg squat position or, ideally, from a standing kick to a near-handstand position. The single-leg squat, described and illustrated here, is recommended as the first step for beginning performers.

Beginners may have difficulty achieving sufficient elevation and maintaining a straight body position during the descent. Lots of support from a good spotter should solve this problem.

Basic Description

(1) Assume a single-leg squat.

(2) Lean forward, place hands on the beam, and extend support leg as you kick other leg upward just beyond a horizontal position. Keep shoulders slightly forward.

(3-4) Join legs, raise one arm out to the side, and lift upper body for descent. Squeeze seat muscles as body lowers and descend with straight or arched body.

(5) Flex knees slightly as you land.

1   2   3   4   5

Kick to Front Vault Dismount

Spotting

Stand on the side of the beam and guide performer to a stand. Support thighs and stomach.

Rear Vault Dismount

Skill Level 1

This is a very basic dismount that affords lots of body contact with the beam and builds confidence.

Basic Description

(1) Sit on the beam sidesaddle style, with one hand on the beam in the rear.

(2-3) Lean back slightly with shoulders and throw legs over the beam. Keep legs joined and extend arm to the side.

(4) Extend hips before landing with slightly bent knees. A half turn may be executed in either direction during the descent.

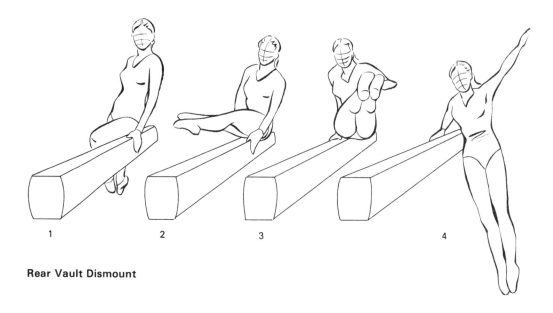

1   2   3   4

Rear Vault Dismount

Spotting

Stand on the side of the beam to the rear of performer. Hold performer's waist and guide her over the beam toward your side.

Round-off Dismount

Skill Level 2

Always try to descend with your body in line with the beam for a good, balanced landing.

Basic Description

(1-2) Kick through a cartwheel position—a quarter turn through a handstand.

(3-5) As body passes through the handstand position, extend shoulders to gain elevation and execute another quarter turn. Keep body straight and hold arms overhead all the way to the landing.

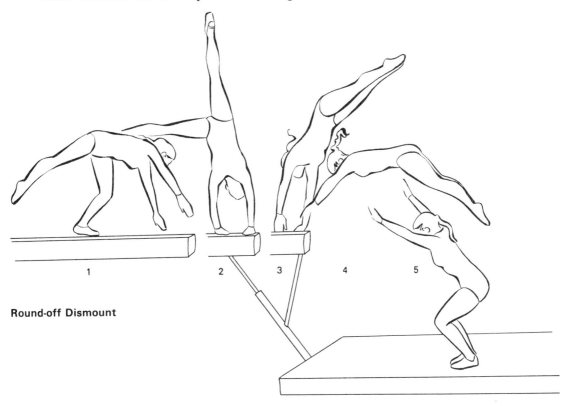

Round-off Dismount

    When your body positions are good enough, you are ready to add a half twist to this dismount. To execute this round-off half twist dismount, push off your hands and turn to the right (if you put your left hand down first for the cartwheel action) as you descend, landing with your back toward the end of

132 the beam. You may also perform a half twist in the opposite direction from the same round-off.

Prerequisites
Round-off on the floor. One-arm (first arm) round-off would be helpful.

Spotting
Stand at the end of the beam on the left side. Place right hand (palm up) under performer's waist as she bends to begin the round-off. After she kicks, place left hand on her waist (other side) and provide support until the landing.

One-Arm Round-off Dismount (End of Beam) (Variation)

Skill Level 2

Keep shoulder over support hand as you pass through the handstand position.

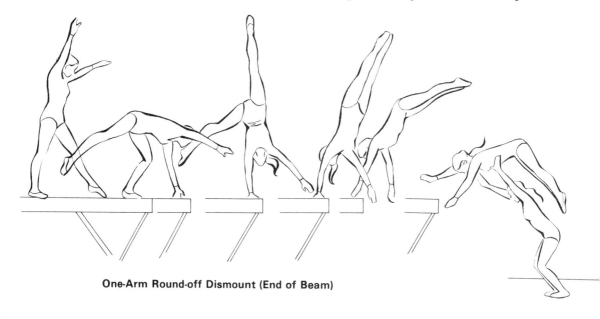

One-Arm Round-off Dismount (End of Beam)

One-Arm Round-off Dismount (Side of Beam) (Variation)

Skill Level 3

Keep shoulder over support hand as you pass through the handstand position. Shift hand position during the last phase to control the landing.

Basic Description

(1) Kick into a round-off on your first arm. Stretch in shoulder area and look down the length of your support arm. Turn head and shoulders in the direction of the rotation.

(2) Join legs and keep hip muscles tight throughout. Do not allow shoulders to lean in any direction as shoulder of free arm completes the turning movement. Extend free arm to the side during the turn to help pull you around.

(3-4) Descend with a straight body. A twist in either direction may be added at this point.

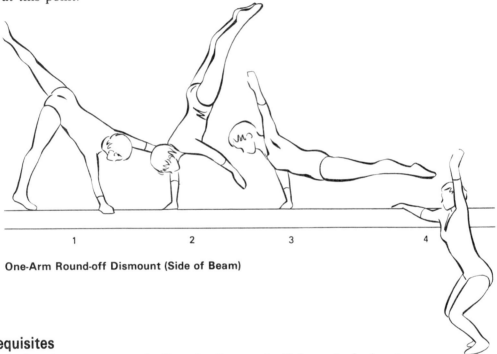

One-Arm Round-off Dismount (Side of Beam)

Prerequisites

Round-off and one-arm round-off on the floor and off the end of a low beam. Practice a side-of-the-beam handstand to an overbalance and into a turn-out dismount to become familiar with the last phase of this skill.

Spotting

Stand on the side of the beam to which performer will land. Support performer's hip as the kick is initiated. Reach around and grasp performer's other hip as soon as the first quarter turn is completed. Move both hands to the waist, once the beam is cleared, and assist the landing.

Cartwheel Dismount

Skill Level 2

Landing sideways has been known to cause knee injuries, and therefore the cartwheel dismount, though not considered difficult, should be avoided, particularly by beginners. A gymnast who decides to practice this skill should protect her knees by adding a quarter twist during the descent (*see* variation) as soon as she learns the basic skill on a crash mat.

Basic Description

(1-4) Kick into a cartwheel, join legs, and push off the beam by stretching in the shoulders. For a lofty cartwheel dismount, push with both arms simultaneously after an aggressive initial kick.

(5-6) Keep body straight and arms extended upward during the descent, and land with slightly bent knees.

Cartwheel Dismount

Spotting

Grasp performer's waist from the rear and control the landing.

Cartwheel Quarter Turn Dismount (Variation)

Skill Level 2

Begin this dismount as you would a round-off or a basic cartwheel dismount. After kicking through the handstand position, push off your right shoulder and execute the twist by giving hips a quarter turn.

Cartwheel Quarter Turn Dismount

Forward Somersault Dismounts

After learning a somersault dismount with the beam at regulation height, alternately perform the skill on low and high settings to counteract the tendency to "dive" onto the mat from the high beam. One session of dismounts from a low beam usually gets the performer back up in the air. Be careful not to over-rotate when performing at regulation height after a session of dismounting from a low beam.

Three basic arm lifts are commonly used in aerial somersault dismounts. The *backward lift* starts with a forward-downward motion and terminates with both arms held rearward and slightly out to the sides. In the *forward lift* the arms are lifted forward-upward from a rearward, behind-the-hips position as the kick occurs. In the *basic lift* (good for learning) the arms begin in an overhead position and are thrown forward-downward and pulled in to the sides (elbows bent) as the kick occurs. This version requires a shoulder shrug (lift) coordinated with the kick.

Aerial Barani Dismount

Skill Level 4

This is the somersault dismount most commonly learned by intermediate performers. It is performed off the end of the beam as described and illustrated here, but may also be executed off the middle of the beam on the left side.

1   2   3

Aerial Barani Dismount

Basic Description

(1-2) Step forward about twenty-four inches with left foot. Bend left knee and hip so that stomach is almost touching thigh. As knee bends, arms begin swinging into a forward or backward lift.

(3) Simultaneously kick right leg overhead and forcefully extend left leg to push off the beam. At this point it is important to be balanced over pushing leg; most beginners lean too far forward in an attempt to get clear of the beam. Do not begin turning head and shoulders as kick and push are executed (although performer in the illustration uses this early-twisting technique); keep body facing forward and attempt to kick "straight over the top" until kicking leg reaches a vertical position. Be sure to finish the push with pushing leg.

(4) Quickly bring left leg up to right leg and turn head and shoulders into the twist.

(5-6) Keep body straight as you descend for the landing.

4   5   6

Prerequisites

Aerial cartwheel on the floor. One-arm round-off dismount on the beam. Practice the aerial barani dismount off a trampoline, using a spotting belt and a crash mat for the landing.

Spotting

Stand to performer's left for an aerial barani twist that is analogous to a left-hand-down-first round-off. Place right hand (palm up) on performer's waist as the initial bend occurs and provide support during the kick. Grasp both sides of performer's waist midway through the skill and support her until she has landed.

Aerial Forward Somersault (Pike or Layout) Dismount

Skill Level 4

This skill is usually executed in a layout or piked position. Avoid leaning too far forward as you push off the beam; it will hamper your ability to lift the somersault. Use a crash mat while learning this skill.

Basic Description

(1-4) Follow the starting procedure for the aerial barani dismount.

(5-7) Join legs and tighten hip muscles. Bring head forward just enough to see the front of your body as you descend; head should not be held far forward in front of upper body. Pike by bringing head and shoulders up toward legs as legs join, or keep body straight as in a handspring to assume a layout position.

(8) Bend knees slightly as you land.

Prerequisites

Aerial walkover on the floor. Aerial forward somersault to a two-foot landing on the trampoline. Forward handspring off the beam.

Spotting

The spotter lifts performer at the beginning, supports the lower back with one hand throughout the somersault, and catches the landing.

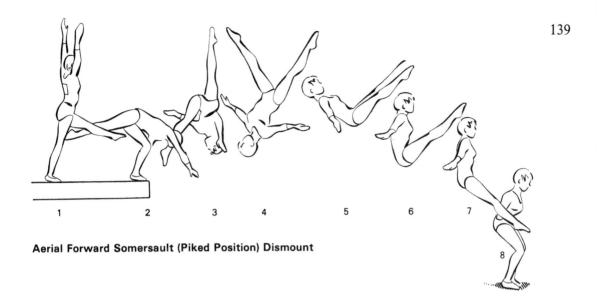

Aerial Forward Somersault (Piked Position) Dismount

Spotting the Aerial Forward Somersault Dismount

Aerial Forward Somersault with Full Twist Dismount

Skill Level 8

This skill is begun like an aerial barani dismount and completed either by continuing into an additional half twist, as illustrated, or by executing a slightly piked aerial forward somersault with a sharp full twist initiated from the pike, the style described here. Follow through with initial leg kick to avoid under-rotating the forward somersault. When learning to add twists to a somersault, there is a tendency to overemphasize the twist at the expense of the somersault.

Basic Description

(1-3) Follow the starting procedure for the aerial barani dismount.

(4-8) Using a forward arm lift, perform an aerial forward somersault with a somewhat rounded back, giving you a slightly piked posture. If you are fast, you will be able to assume this position immediately after the inverted vertical position. At this point, quickly extend hips and execute a twist by pulling one shoulder backward and throwing other arm across chest in the direction of the twist. Keep arms close to body after the twist is begun.

(9-11) Prior to the landing, extend arms to the side to slow the twist. Land with slightly bent knees.

Aerial Forward Somersault with Full Twist Dismount

Prerequisite

Slightly piked aerial forward somersault off the beam.

Spotting

This skill should be practiced on the trampoline with an overhead spotting belt; it will greatly facilitate learning the correct action for the somersault and the twist.

To spot a late-twisting somersault, stand on the side that corresponds to the direction of the twist. Place arm under performer's back as she executes the twist, and allow her to roll on your arm as you support her landing. Some coaches prefer to stand on the other side and thrust performer's hips into the full twist with an arm-flipping action. To spot an early-twisting somersault, spot the first half twist by placing one hand under performer's waist as in the initial phase of the aerial barani spotting technique. Then, instead of grasping both sides of performer's waist as you would in spotting the barani, grasp her hip and pull it upward "over the top" into the last half of the twist. Keep in mind that, if the early-twisting technique is used, the performer must be taught to execute a right twist if the barani movement is analogous to a left round-off, and vice-versa. Otherwise you will be spotting an attempt to twist in two different directions.

7 8 9 10 11

Backward Somersault Dismounts

Backward somersault dismounts are executed by using the same tumbling techniques employed in performing other balance beam skills. The additional elevation provided by the beam generally makes backward (and forward) somersault dismounts somewhat easier to perform than their counterparts in the floor exercise event. Any problem a performer may have in executing a backward somersault (provided she can execute the skill on the floor) is usually the result of the restrictions imposed on foot placement during the takeoff, fear of hitting the beam, or fear of elevation.

Fear of elevation can be overcome by surrounding the beam with piled-up crash mats and removing one mat a day, or by gradually raising the beam from a low position. Anxiety about elevation is often directly related to fear of hitting the beam and to the problem of foot placement. These fears must be controlled through repetition, which leads to gradual improvement and increasing confidence. It is recommended that all backward somersault dismount skills be learned on the trampoline first. If a trampoline is not available, use spotting platforms, spotting belts, piled-up mats, or other training aids to increase safety.

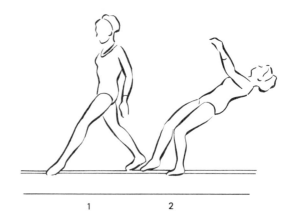

1   2

Backward Handspring Dismount

Backward Handspring Dismount

Skill Level 5

Although it is not a backward somersault, this skill resembles a backward somersault dismount enough to be included in this category.

Basic Description

(1-3) Take a big step forward with arms held behind hips. Kick rear leg upward (slightly off to the side of the beam) as you throw arms backward into the handspring.

(4-7) Look for the beam as you put hand down for support. (Bring both hands down on the beam until you can do it with one.) Keep support shoulder over support hand and join legs for the landing.

Prerequisites

Backward walkover on the beam and a backward walkover into a dismount. Backward handspring on the floor. Backward handspring on the beam is also desirable.

Spotting

Use an overhead spotting belt. Otherwise, stand on the side of the beam and spot performer to a landing into a crash mat until one arm can be substituted for two.

3   4   5   6   7

Tucked Gainer Backward Somersault Dismount

Skill Level 6

Basic Description

(1-3) Step forward with arms held behind hips. Kick rear leg upward as you lean backward off-balance, and lift arms overhead. Follow through with leg kick before allowing your head to move backward.

(4-6) Pull knees over your shoulders (tuck), keeping your head in a neutral position but looking for the floor as you come around. Release the tuck as body completes its rotation.

(7-9) Extend before landing. You may grasp the beam as early as possible for stability while learning.

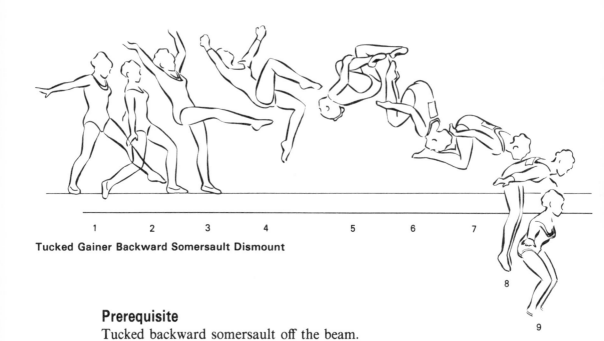

Tucked Gainer Backward Somersault Dismount

Prerequisite

Tucked backward somersault off the beam.

Spotting

A belt spot is strongly advised. Hand-spot from the right side on elevated crash mats so that you are almost level with the beam. Reach under performer's back with right hand as she kicks. Place left hand on her stomach and help turn her over to her feet.

Layout Backward Somersault Dismount

Skill Level 7

This dismount may be performed off the side as well as the end of the beam.

Basic Description
(1-3) Precede the somersault with a cartwheel (optional).
(4-5) From a slight bend in hips and knees, jump backward with a forceful arm thrust.
(6-7) Tighten seat muscles and straighten your back as much as possible. (The performer in the illustration is somewhat over-arched.) Bring arms toward hips briskly to improve rotation.
(8-9) Pike down slightly and land with slightly bent knees.

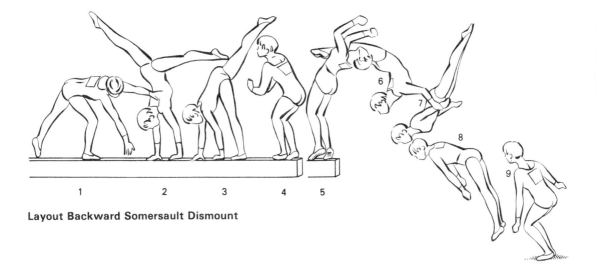

Layout Backward Somersault Dismount

Prerequisites
Backward handspring on the floor. Tucked backward somersault dismount from the beam.

Spotting
Place right hand on lower back while standing on performer's right side, and assist the jump. Place left hand on her stomach halfway through the somersault to provide support. Assist the landing.

Backward Somersault with Full Twist Dismount (End of Beam)

Skill Level 8

The basic technique used in the full twisting backward somersault is the same whether this skill is performed off the end or off the side of the beam. Executing this dismount off the side is somewhat more difficult because the performer must thrust sideways as well as backward. The two illustrations that follow demonstrate both versions of this skill from different perspectives.

Basic Description

(1-2) With knees and hips slightly bent, jump upward and vigorously throw arms overhead, holding them rather wide apart. Thrust arms to at least shoulder level before allowing head to move backward. As the takeoff occurs the hips are slightly behind feet and right hip is elevated.

(3-5) The arms are brought in sharply toward the body and inclined in the direction of the twist. Turn head in the direction of the twist and watch the mat below. Keep hip muscles tight throughout.

(6) Hold arms to the sides away from body to slow the twisting action. Bend hips in preparation for the landing.

Prerequisites

Layout backward somersault from the beam. Some experience performing a full twisting backward somersault on floor or trampoline.

Spotting

The overhead spotting belt is recommended. Hand-spot on the right side of performer from a platform. As performer jumps and twists right, reach under her stomach with right forearm and provide support. Reach over her back and grasp right side of her waist with left hand. Turn and support performer through the last half of the twist and assist her landing.

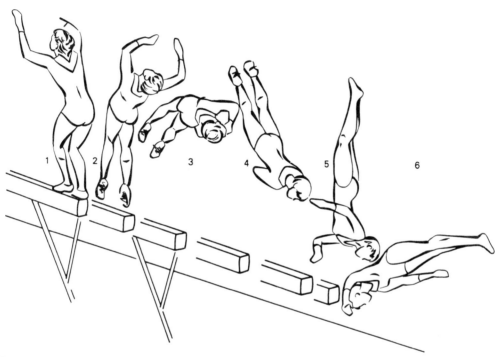

Backward Somersault with Full Twist Dismount (End of Beam)

Backward Somersault with Full Twist Dismount (Side of Beam) (Variation)

Skill Level 8

This illustration shows how the preceding dismount skill is performed off the side of the beam, and offers a different perspective.

Backward Somersault with Full Twist Dismount (Side of Beam)

ROUTINES ON THE BALANCE BEAM

The following illustrations demonstrate routine composition on the balance beam, with the skills numbered consecutively. The first is an intermediate routine that incorporates many simple movements. Except for the walkover, needle scale, and dismount, this routine is rather basic. The second and third routines are championship routines that demonstrate a very high level of performance. Many of the skills and combinations used in these routines may be modified in some fashion to fit an intermediate level performance. Study the combinations and choose some movements that you will be able to use in your routine.

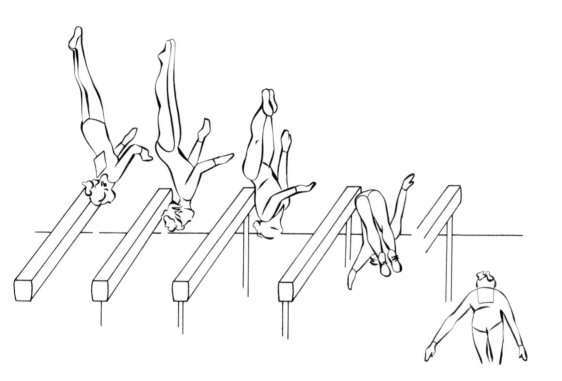

Intermediate Routine

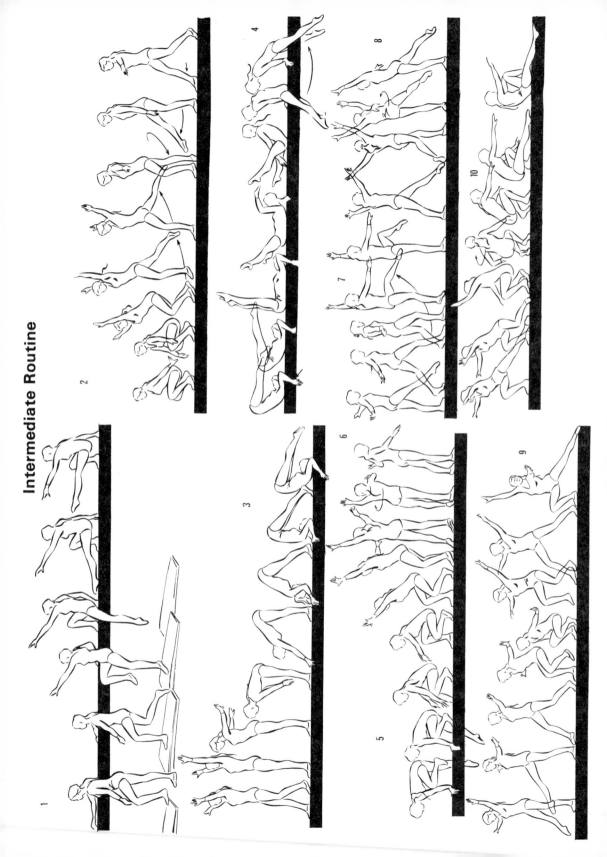

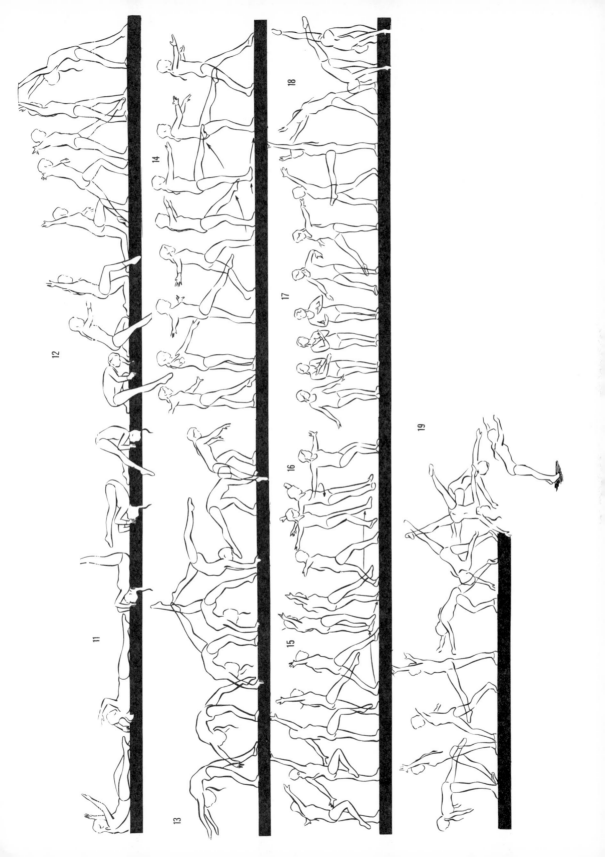

Advanced Routine

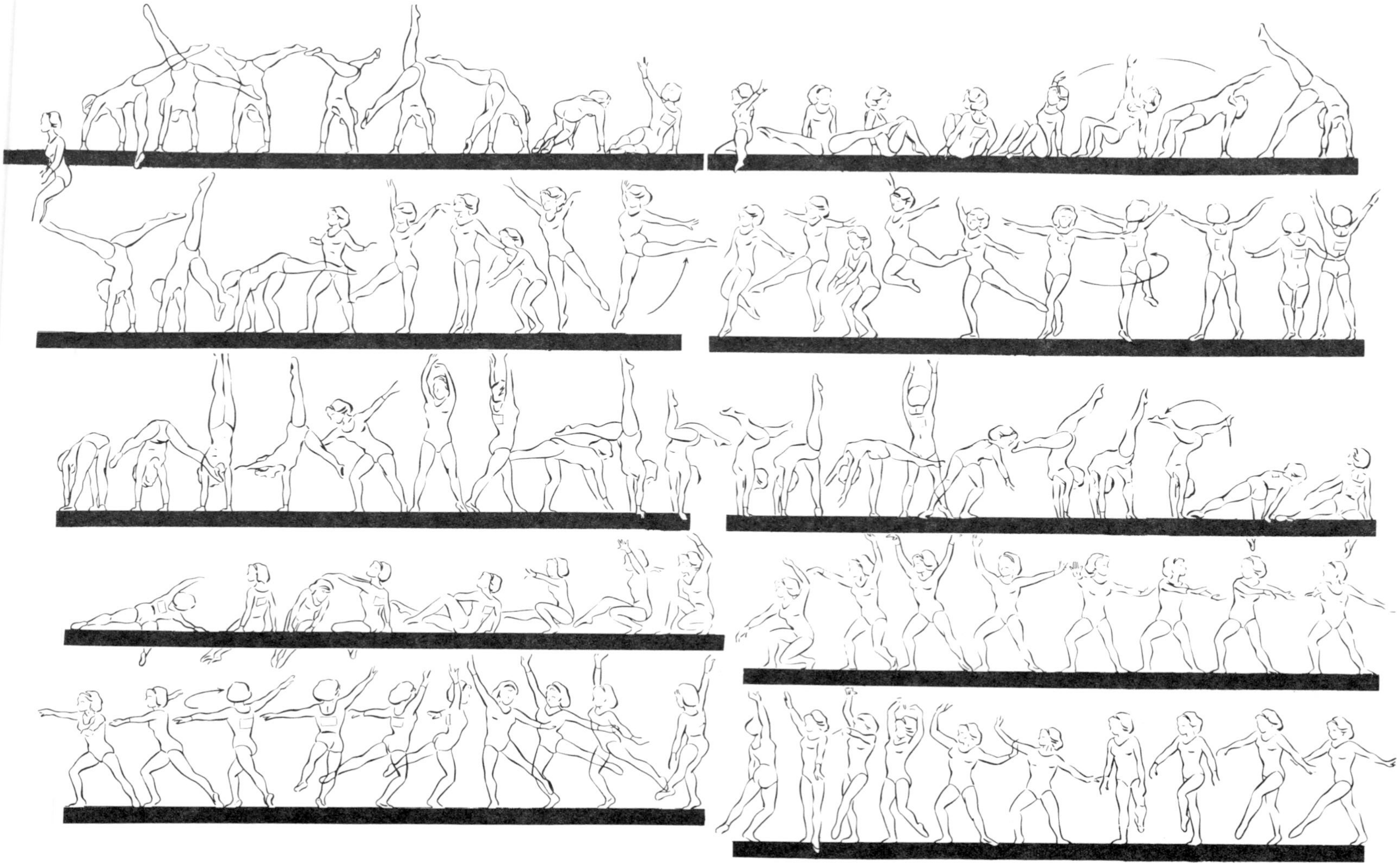

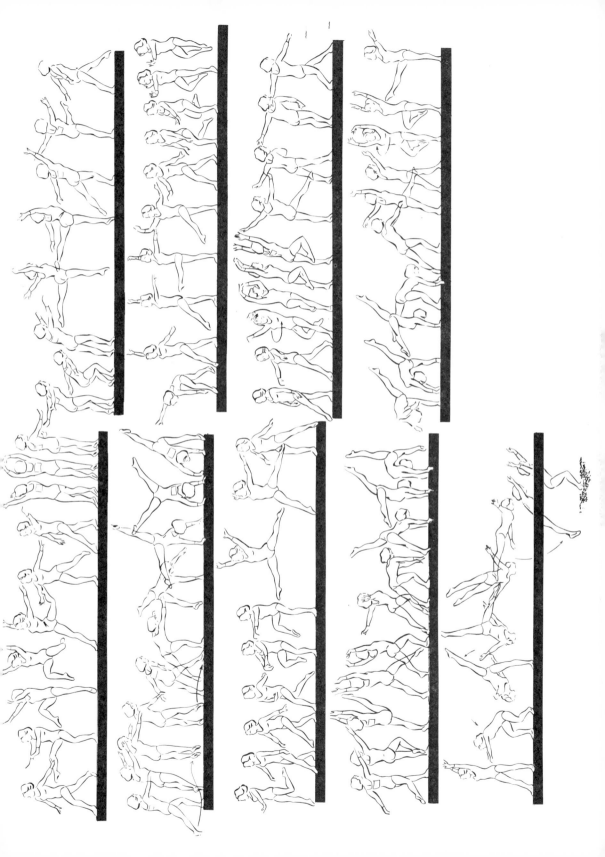

Advanced Routine

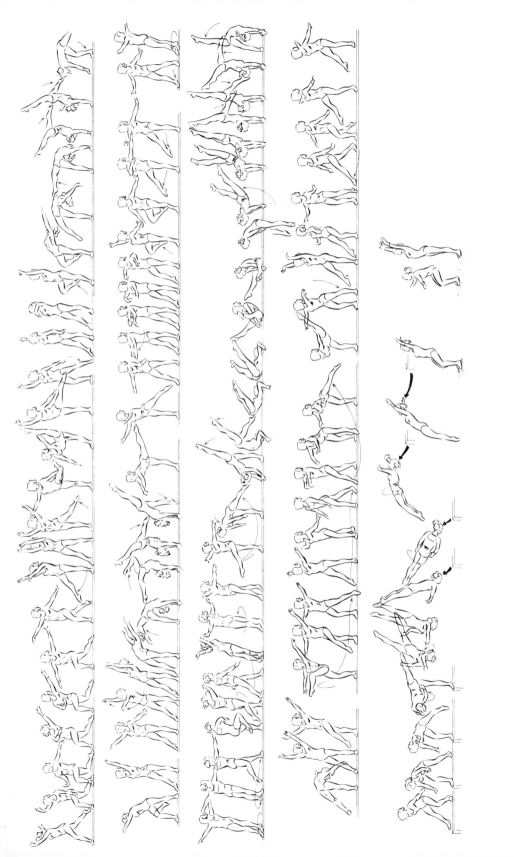

3

Uneven Parallel Bars

Brief History

The uneven parallel bars event is one of the fastest-moving and most difficult events in women's gymnastics. A complete routine, consisting of approximately fifteen elements, lasts only about twenty seconds. The parallel bars performer must have strength, coordination, and agility to hop, cast, pirouette, and move from bar to bar without stopping for a rest.

Prior to the early 1950's, both men and women performed on the *even* parallel bars. Women competed on slightly narrower and lower adjustments to accommodate their smaller frames. Although women competitors usually performed more double support skills (arm and leg support at the same time) than men, the best women gymnasts took pride in mastering the more strenuous male-oriented skills. During this period, the two wooden rails were oval-shaped, short, stiff, and always varnished. During the mid-1950's, one bar was raised and the other was lowered to create uneven parallel bars for the women's event. Over the years, the bars have been lengthened and rounded for greater flexibility and gripping power.

157

At first, the skills performed in the new, uneven parallel bars event consisted of static poses, handstands, hip and leg circles, and various climbing skills. Imagination and years of training eventually brought about the development of "hop" changes from the feet, hands, and hips, along with a style requiring constant movement.

Today's rules dictate an aggressive, non-stop performance of swinging skills that cannot be duplicated in any other event.

Spotting

It is advisable to spot all skills performed by a beginner. The spotter must stand in the correct position for each skill and support, pull, or push at the proper time and place. In some cases, it is wise to have two spotters to guarantee safety.

The performer and the spotter should decide together whether a particular skill requires assistance. If aid is required, the next consideration is whether to assist to insure safety, to help the gymnast perform the skill, or to fulfill both functions at the same time.

The spotter should always focus on the performer's center of gravity—the approximate middle of her body—as she moves from bar to bar. If it is possible that the performer will slip off the bar at a certain point, the spotter's arms should be under the performer before that point is reached. The spotter must be one step ahead of the performer at all times.

As the gymnast becomes more proficient in performing a skill, spotting may be decreased. When the performer is completely confident, self-reliant, and a hundred percent consistent, spotting the skill is no longer necessary.

Protecting the Hands

Everyone who practices this event experiences torn hands (broken blisters) from time to time. Start slowly, beginning with short training sessions and building up to longer workouts. Your hands will toughen up over a period of time. Do not put an excessive amount of tape on your hands; it may inhibit your gripping power. If you do rip your hands, treat the injury as you would any minor cut. Clean the blisters, bandage them, and suspend training for a while.

Many performers wear hand guards made of leather, wick, or gauze. The most popular type of hand guard is made of soft leather and has a non-slip buckle that allows easy adjustment. These are designed to fit the hand snugly to improve the grip and retard tearing of the hands. Most hand guards require two or three training sessions before they conform exactly to the shape of the hand. Begin breaking in new hand guards as your old ones become worn. Make sure your hand guards fit well, and check them frequently for premature tearing.

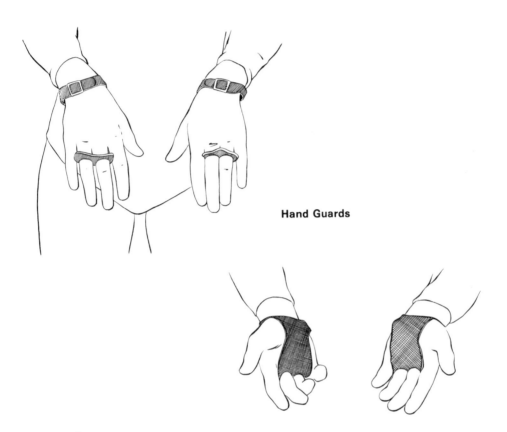

Hand Guards

Training Clothing

A leotard is best; bulky clothes may get caught on the bar as you perform.

Routine Composition

Mount
Start with a run or mount from a stand. Either bar may be grasped from any direction.

Variety of Movement

If a skill must be repeated, it should never be repeated with the same connecting skills. Perform at least two twisting skills.

Continuity

Each skill should lead smoothly into the ensuing one with no extraneous movements that are unrelated to the skill that follows. The routine should flow with no pauses.

Levels

The performer should change levels frequently and not perform more than three skills in succession on one bar.

Hops

Simultaneous grip changes are considered exciting; from four to six of these should be incorporated into every routine.

Surprise

Originality always makes a routine more interesting.

Dismount

Try not to hesitate or stop before executing a dismount unless it is essential for safety. The dismount should be one of your more difficult skills to insure that your routine ends impressively.

Post-training Exercises

The uneven parallel bars event requires more all-around strength than the other women's Olympic gymnastic events because most of the skills are performed with an aggressive pulling or pushing action. The stomach muscles must be particularly strong to lift the legs into position for kips and casts. Most serious bar performers include post-training exercises in their schedules to strengthen the upper body. Consult *Women's Gymnastics 1* for information about special conditioning exercises.

Grips

Every skill requires a particular grip or series of grips. A wrong grip often changes the style of the skill and can be dangerous. As a general rule, use an over grip when circling backward and an under grip when circling forward. A forward hip circle (for which an over grip is used) is perhaps the only exception to this rule.

Double Over Grip

The palms face away from you. The thumbs may be held below the bar or alongside the other fingers.

Double Under Grip

The palms face you. The thumbs may be wrapped around the bar or held alongside the other fingers.

Mixed Grip

A combination of over and under grips.

Crossed Mixed Grip

The arms are crossed at the wrists with over and under grips.

Eagle Grip

The arms are held rearward-upward with the palms of the hands turned out away from the body and over the bar.

Double Over Grip

Double Under Grip

Mixed Grip

Crossed Mixed Grip

Eagle Grip

Basic Positions

Most of the terms used to describe positions and skills on the uneven bars have evolved over the years in a very disorganized fashion. In general, American gymnasts and coaches have adopted men's horizontal bar terms to describe uneven bars skills and basic positions. In this chapter, standard (common) terminology is used whenever possible; however, new names for several heretofore unnamed basic positions will be introduced.

Hangs

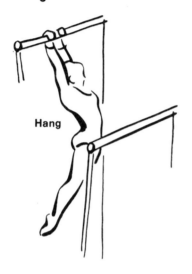

Hang

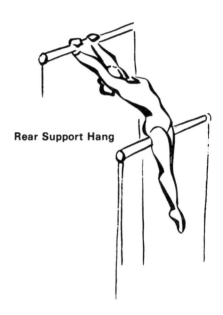

Rear Support Hang

Straddle Inverted Hang

Knee Hang

163

Front Support Hang

Piked Front Support Hang

Wrap Support Hang

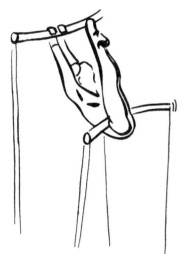

Piked Inverted Hang

Front Support

Free Front Support

Free-Arm Front Support

Free "L" Rear Support

Piked Front Support

Rear Support

Free Piked ("V") Rear Support (1)

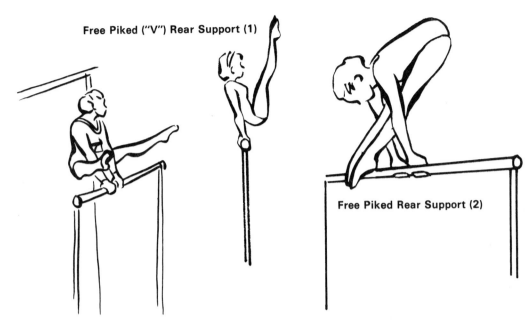

Free Piked Rear Support (2)

Free Straddle "L" Support

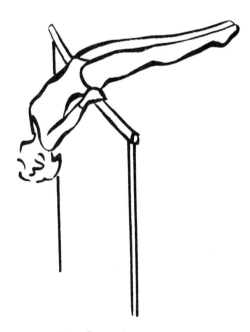

Layout Rear Support

Inverted Double Front Support

Inverted Double Rear Support

Inverted Support (Handstand)

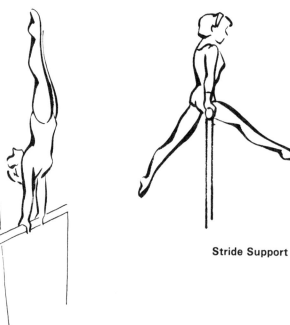

Stride Support

Stands

Piked Support Stand

Straddle Support Stand

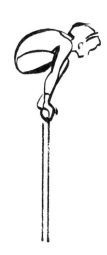

Squat Support Stand

Hanging

You will be assuming the following hang positions often throughout your training, so be sure that you can perform them without strain.

Straight Hang

One of the first things the beginner should learn is to hang with trunk and shoulders stretched. This is a straight body hang with *hips tucked under* (stomach in) for a straight-line effect. The head should always be aligned with the upper body.

Correct Straight Hang

Hang on the bar, relax in the shoulders, and let gravity pull you into a straight line.

Incorrect Straight Hang

Do not arch your lower back, pull up in the shoulders, or thrust your head forward while in a straight hang position.

Arched Hang

Assume a straight hang and arch your lower back only, keeping your seat muscles tight.

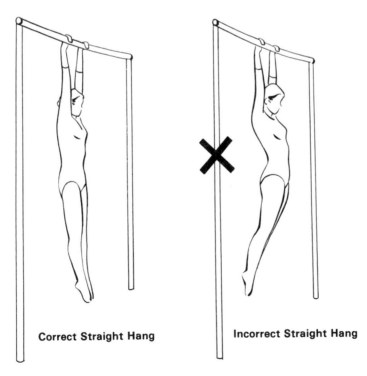

Correct Straight Hang   **Incorrect Straight Hang**

Correct Arched Hang

Arch your back with your seat muscles tensed, shoulders extended, and head aligned with upper body.

Incorrect Arched Hang

Do not relax your seat muscles, pull up in the shoulders, or thrust your head forward.

Piked Hang

Assume a straight hang and raise your legs (keeping them straight) into a slightly piked position with your hips tucked under.

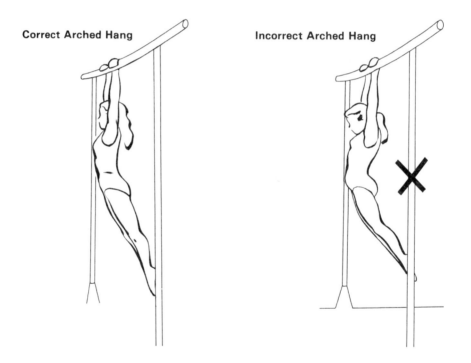

Correct Arched Hang   Incorrect Arched Hang

Correct Piked Hang

Always lift your legs with your lower back held flat. Keep your hips tucked under, shoulders stretched, and head aligned with your upper body.

Do not let your seat protrude, duck your head, or pull up in the shoulders.

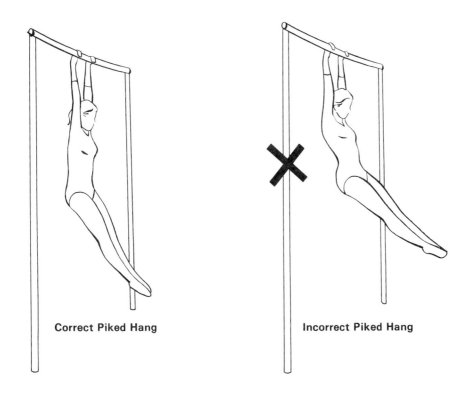

Correct Piked Hang   Incorrect Piked Hang

Swinging

Assume a straight hang. Quickly lift your legs into a piked position with your hips tucked under, and create a swing. Arch your back (keep seat muscles tight) after you pass through the straight body position at the base of the swing. Swing back and forth, emphasizing shoulder stretch and correct hip action.

Basic Movements

Casting off Bar from Front Support Position

Skill Level 1

The speed of your cast off the bar determines how high your legs rise in the rear. This basic movement is used in many skills.

Basic Description

Assume a front support position with head aligned with upper body, shoulders down, and hips tucked under (seat muscles tensed). Your upper thighs will probably be resting against the bar.

(1) Pike (hips tucked under, stomach held in) as you bend elbows slightly to place the bar just under hip bones.

(2-3) Whip legs backward through a straight body position into an arched position, keeping hip muscles tight. This action will cause hips to fly off the bar if you coordinate it properly with an arm push. Try to get the feel of the bend of the bar as you pike and cast. The rebound action of the bar should be used to help you gain elevation. After the cast has been established, remove the arch from your lower back and assume a straight body position.

Gliding

Skill Level 3

The basic glide swing below the bar requires a fair amount of abdominal and hip flexor muscle strength. Practice this action several times at the end of each training session. Almost every top routine employs a glide action into a kip, overshoot, or half-turn combination.

Gliding

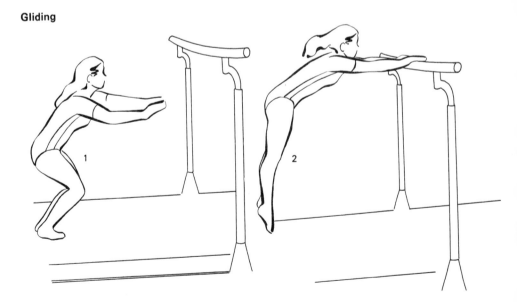

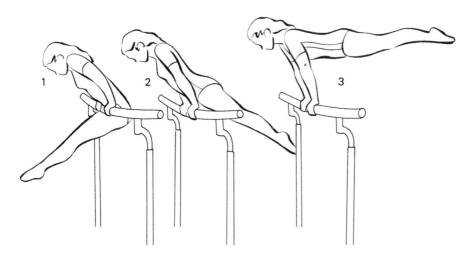

Casting off Bar from Front Support Position

Basic Description

(1-5) Jump and glide with arms aligned with upper body. Your hips should be tucked under (lower back kept flat) as you pike to keep feet from hitting the mat. As shoulders pass the bottom of the swing, open the pike to assume a straight body position, and keep hip muscles tight.

1   2   3

Swinging in a Piked Inverted Hang

Skill Level 3

Numerous skills stem from a swing in a piked inverted hang position. Learn this movement by hanging in this position and pumping your seat in one direction and shooting your legs in the other until you can generate swing.

Basic Description

(1-5) From a rear support position, pull legs up to a "V" position and pull hips down in a tight piked swing. Rock under the bar, then swing back and shoot over the bar to your original rear support position. Make a special effort to pull shoulders upward as you shoot legs over the bar; otherwise you will finish hanging by your hips and hands below the bar.

You may want to perform a more elementary version of this skill, at first. In this case, jump, grasp the bar, and assume the piked inverted hang position

4   5

by passing both legs between your arms. Pump into a swing by leading with your seat as you rotate backward and opening the pike slightly as you rise. The higher you can pull yourself at each end of the swing, without touching the bars, the better your swing will be.

Hip-lifting off the Bar

Skill Level 1

Many skills on the bars require a hip-lift "popping" action to create enough force to propel the performer into the air for a dismount or hop change skill. This core movement should be learned as a separate skill.

Your speed in opening (straightening) your body from the piked position will determine the distance you are propelled upward, and your balance will determine the direction of the "pop." This movement punishes the hips, so be sure to use a bar pad for protection. Spotting is also advisable.

Basic Description

   (1) From a front support position, pike and hang over the bar. Generate a slight rocking motion by gently swinging arms and legs.

(2-4) Quickly lift upper body and legs to a momentary arched position. If your lift is fast and your balance is correct, you will be able to pop off the low bar to a stand on the mat under the high bar. Be sure to open from the pike at the movement your slight swing is rotating backward so that you can project yourself to the rear of the low bar.

Hip-lifting off the Bar

UNEVEN PARALLEL BARS SKILLS

Jump to Front Support on Low Bar

Skill Level 1

Beginners will find that holding the body straight with tight seat muscles in a front support position on one bar is no easy task. Once the degree of forward lean and the placement of the bar on your thighs has been determined, you will learn the position quickly.

    This technique is often used as a mount prior to executing any skill that rotates backward from a free (thighs not touching the bar) front support. Try this movement with a run and jump (from a vaulting board) to a free front support.

Basic Description

(1) Stand with hands (over grips) on the bar.

(2-3) Bend knees and jump to a front support position with hip muscles (seat and stomach) held tight. Hold shoulders down and keep head in line with upper body. The bar will probably be resting on your thighs and you will have to lean forward to hold a balanced position.

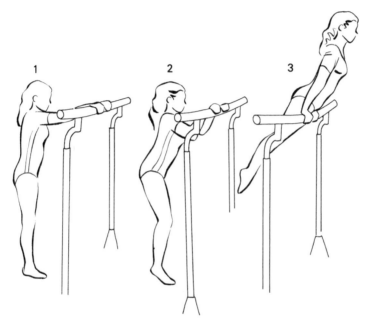

Jump to Front Support on Low Bar

Prerequisite

Ability to jump to and hold a front support.

Spotting

Stand on the side of performer and guide her into position by holding upper arm and legs. Adjust performer's body position.

Single-Leg Cut on Low Bar

Skill Level 1

Before trying the leg cut, practice shifting your weight from arm to arm while raising the opposite leg. Push down on the bar and release, for an instant, as you raise your leg.

Basic Description

(1-4) From a front support position, bend hips and cast one leg forward over the bar and under one hand, at the same time shifting your weight to the other arm. Quickly regrasp the bar in a stride support position, and keep thigh and hip muscles tight.

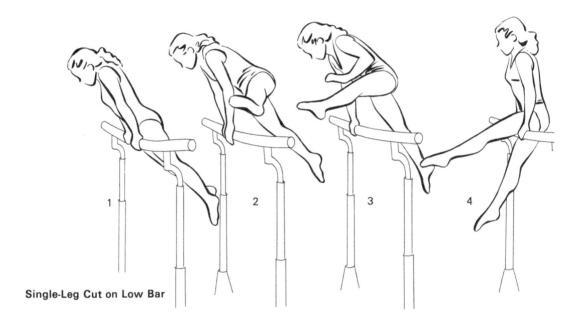

Single-Leg Cut on Low Bar

Prerequisites

Ability to hold a front support and stride support.

Spotting

Stand on the side opposite cutting leg and hold support arm with both hands. One hand supports upper arm and the other holds wrist. Keep support arm from over-leaning or buckling.

Single-Leg Turn on Low Bar

Skill Level 1

The beginning gymnast should practice turning on one bar with her knees and toes very straight at all times. Try to execute this short series of movements without stopping or sagging in the shoulders. This turn will help you learn to shift your weight. It also comes in handy when you have to turn around in the middle of a routine.

Basic Description

(1) Assume a front support position with left hand in an under-grip position.

(2-5) Lean to the left and swing right leg over the bar as right hand releases the bar. Regrasp the bar with right hand.

(6-9) Release right hand, turn to the left, and regrasp the bar with right hand as illustrated. The backs of upper thighs rest on the bar during the turn.

(10-12) Swing left leg over the bar to the rear and assume a front support position.

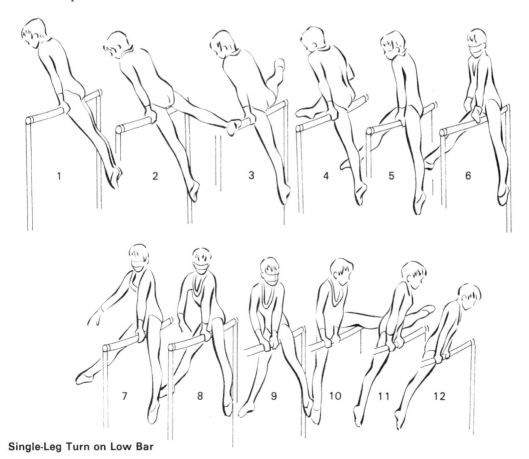

Single-Leg Turn on Low Bar

Prerequisite

Single-leg cut from a front support.

Spotting

Support performer's support arm for the first cut. Support both arms from the front for the turn.

Backward Pullover on Low and High Bar

Skill Level 1

Beginners often have difficulty kicking their legs over the bar and pulling up with their arms at the same time. Sufficient arm and abdominal strength, keeping your head forward, and watching your toes usually solves this problem. On the low bar, the pullover is begun with a *sustained* push by the pushing leg. On the high bar, the legs join after the hips have contacted the bar. Pull with your arms enough to bring your hips to rest on the bar at just the right point for the front support position at the end. Learn to perform this skill from a stand on the floor and from a single-leg rear support hang on the low bar. The basic movement of this skill is much the same on both bars. The second version will provide you with an introduction to the high bar.

Basic Description

Low Bar

(1-5) Stand with hands on the low bar (over grips) and bend arms. Hold one leg to the rear, then swing it forward swiftly and kick leg over the bar while pulling with arms continuously. The arms should not straighten as they pull. Watch legs join as they go over the bar. Raise upper body, straighten arms, and assume a front support position with hip muscles tight.

High Bar

Assume a rear support hang position.

(1-4) Bend one knee and place the ball of the foot on the low bar. Push down on the low bar sharply with bent leg and kick straight leg over the high bar while pulling with arms. Watch legs as they join and pass over the bar. Raise upper body, straighten arms, and assume a front support position with tight hips.

Prerequisites

Ability to hang with arms bent for several seconds (pulling power). Ability to kick and join legs at bar level.

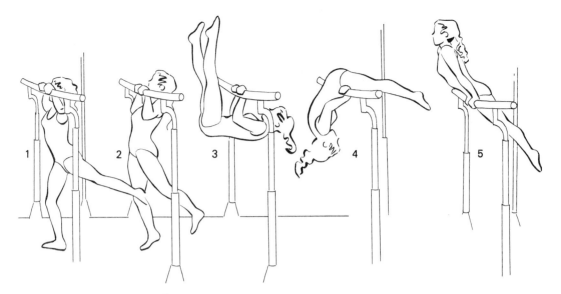

Backward Pullover on Low Bar

Backward Pullover on High Bar

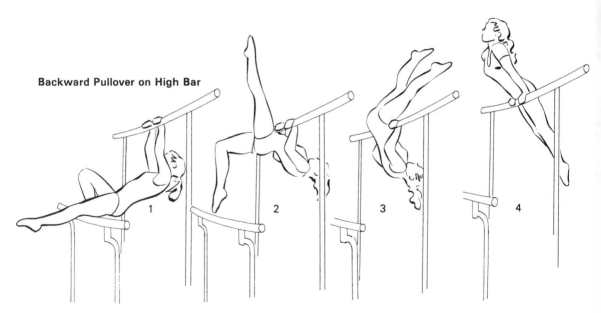

Spotting

Low Bar

Stand on the side of performer and behind the bar. Support and guide performer's upper back with one hand and legs with other hand. Assist the front support position.

High Bar

Stand under the high bar. Support performer's upper back and hips as she kicks over the bar. Grasp performer's ankles and steady her.

Single-Knee Swing-up

Skill Level 1

This skill requires a rocking action that is a little tricky for some beginners to learn. While practicing this skill, wear an elastic wrap around your knee to avoid bruising the back of your bent leg. This is mainly a low-bar recovery skill; it is one of the easiest ways to get above the low bar from a hanging position, allowing the performer to continue her routine without getting off the apparatus

Single-Knee Swing-up

and beginning again. One is rarely faced with this problem on the high bar because of the availability of the low bar for use as an additional support.

Try this skill from a stride support position as well, swinging down under the bar and back up to a stride support.

Basic Description
(1) Hang below the low bar with over grips, put one leg between arms, and bend knee over the bar. The other leg is held straight.

(2-6) Place straight leg close to the bar and swing it downward hard. As swinging leg approaches the floor, pull with arms to get shoulders over the bar. Once upper body is entirely above the bar, assume a stride support position.

Leg-cast over Low Bar from Hang on High Bar

Skill Level 1

You will have to move quickly to perform this skill. If you arch your back correctly in the beginning, you will be able to lift your legs high as you swing forward. You can perform this movement as a mount or in the middle of your routine. If you use it as a mount, you must jump from behind the high bar, raise your legs as soon as your hands touch the bar, and cast them forward over the low bar with a piking movement. You should learn this skill in the tucked, straddle, and piked positions, in that order. You may also cast one leg over the bar to end in a stride support position.

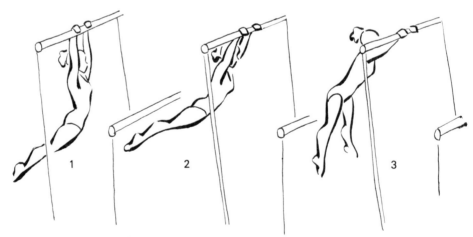

Leg-cast over Low Bar from Hang on High Bar

Basic Description

(1) Stand under the high bar and jump to a hang on the bar.

(2-7) Arch lower back aggressively and pull legs sharply upward and over the low bar to a rear support hang position. Your legs will probably hit the low bar if you use the piked position; in this case, swing to the rear before you arch, giving you more room between legs and the low bar.

Prerequisite

Ability to hang in an "L" position for several seconds.

Spotting

Help performer lift her legs by supporting her lower back and legs from the side. Step in from the rear when spotting the straddle-over.

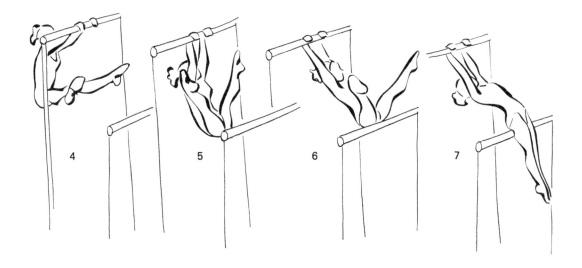

4   5   6   7

Double-Leg Back Rise to High Bar

Skill Level 1

This is approximately the same movement as jumping from the floor to a front support on the low bar. However, in this instance the jump propels the body backward, which complicates matters slightly. Practice this skill with the bars set rather close together until you have the feel of the leg push and arm pull. Follow through with your leg push and bend your arms only slightly. Try to execute this skill in one smooth motion. When you have mastered it, attempt it from a hang on the high bar.

Basic Description

(1) Hang on the high bar with over grips, hands spread wider than the width of your hips. Bend knees and place the balls of both feet on the low bar. Keep arms straight.

(2-3) Push with legs until they are straight and simultaneously pull down with slightly bent arms to raise shoulders over the high bar.

Prerequisite

Jump to a front support on the low bar from a stand on the mat.

Spotting

Stand between the bars and grasp performer's ankle and the back of her thigh. As performer pushes with legs, push upward and assist throughout.

Double-Leg Back Rise to High Bar

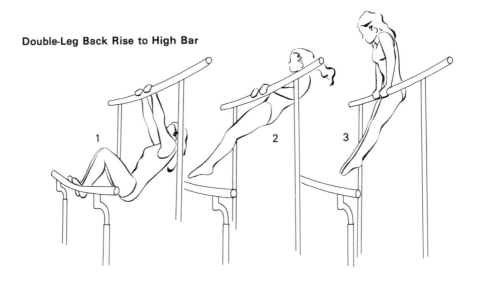

1   2   3

Single-Leg Back Rise to High Bar

Skill Level 1

This skill is executed using the same basic technique employed in performing the double-leg back rise, except that here one leg is held straight and raised to a position close to the high bar. Most beginners have difficulty keeping their high leg close to the high bar as they push with the other leg. If this is a problem, the bars should be set a little closer together.

Basic Description

(1-5) Raise straight leg so that ankle is brought close to the high bar. Push with bent leg and pull upward with arms. At the same time, "step out" with straight leg, thrusting it upward and outward in front of the high bar all the way to the hip and then downward as upper body is pulled above the bar. Finish in a front support position.

Single-Leg Back Rise to High Bar

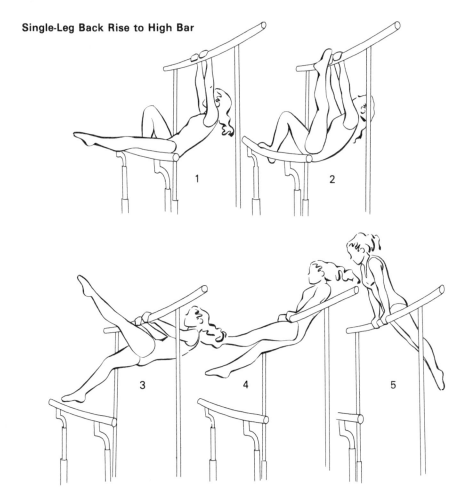

Prerequisites

Jump from the floor to a front support on the low bar. Double-leg back rise to the high bar.

Spotting

Grasp ankle and thigh of bent leg. Push thigh upward and support ankle.

Forward Stride Circle; Forward Stride Circle Catch High Bar

Skill Level 2

This skill is executed with a double under grip, as are all forward circling skills except the forward hip circle. To avoid the errors most commonly committed by beginners, be sure to reach well forward with your front leg and do not hunch your upper body as you start. Also, it is better to miss this skill with your legs straight than to bend your front knee over the bar and try to struggle up to your original position on top of the bar.

See glide to a single-leg overshoot, a related skill.

Basic Description

(1-2) Assume a stride support position. You may place either leg forward.

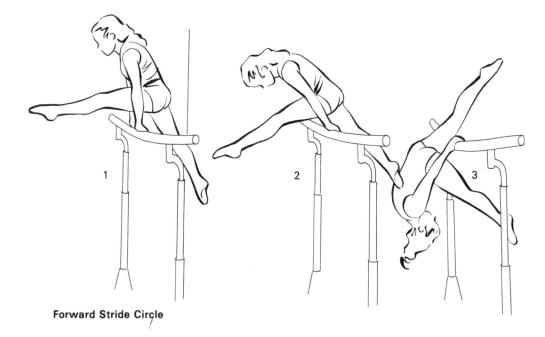

Forward Stride Circle

Raise forward leg as if to take a giant step forward, keeping thigh and hip muscles of both legs very tight. Simultaneously, push down with arms (depress shoulders) and lean forward. Keep upper body nearly straight and do not hunch forward.

(3-6) Circle the bar. Do not let knees bend. When shoulders are about even with the bar, pull them forward over the bar without bending arms, or, to execute the catch, release the low bar and catch the high bar.

Prerequisites

For the release-and-catch: forward stride circle with excellent control. For the stride circle without the release-and-catch: all basics preceding this skill.

Spotting

Stand to the rear of the bar and to the left side of performer. Reach under the bar with left hand and grasp performer's wrist with your thumb down. Hold performer's wrist to the bar while moving with the circle. Reach under performer's lower back and support it with your right hand. When spotting the release-and-catch, release performer's wrist when she has completed three-quarters of a circle and catch her waist with both hands. The performer may hit the spotter during her grip change, so be prepared to back up quickly before moving in for the catch.

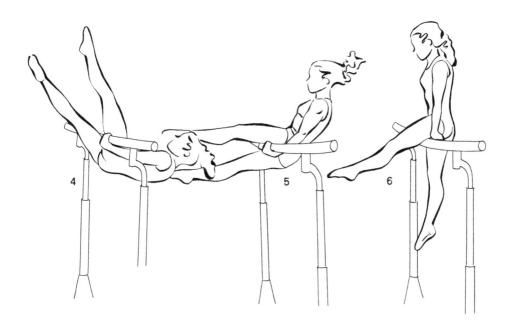

Cast from Front Support Position

Skill Level 1

All skills that circle backward from a front support are preceded by a casting of the hips away from the bar. Take the time to learn this skill. (*See* instructions and illustration for casting off the bar from a front support position earlier in this chapter.)

Cast to Straddle Stand (Variation)

Skill Level 2

Cast as high as possible before straddling to a stand. Straddle legs close to hands and stretch in the shoulders. To lengthen your body for the downswing, push out in the shoulders as you stand on the bar. The balls of your feet should rest lightly on the bar. A spotter should stabilize your shoulders while you are learning this skill.

Cast to Straddle Stand

Front Support Hang and Cast to Straddle over Low Bar to Hang on High Bar (Variation)

Skill Level 3

Adjust the distance between the bars so that the lower bar fits your bent hips in the hang position. Quickly pike as much as possible and cast legs backward-upward; do not pull up your shoulders. Perform a good cast before straddling legs. Straddle legs and pike over the low bar as you swing down. You may have to pull up in the shoulders slightly to keep your seat from hitting the low bar. Straighten hips immediately after passing over the low bar.

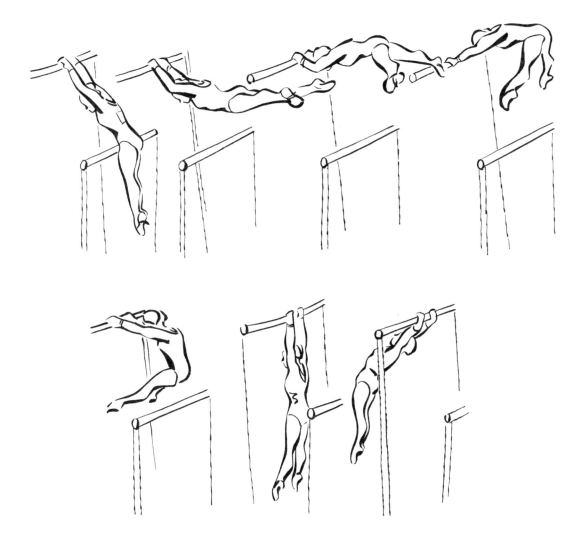

Front Support Hang and Cast to Straddle over Low Bar to Hang on High Bar

Cast to Handstand (Variation)

Skill Level 8

Keep arms straight and hip muscles tight. The cast to a handstand with the body kept straight demonstrates the highest degree of casting ability. This movement can be made easier by assuming a piked straddle position after the cast off the bar. Strong casting power, forward shoulder lean, and an arm-push from the shoulders are required for this skill. Practice it on the low bar with a spotter thrusting your hips and stabilizing your shoulders.

Backward Hip Circle

Skill Level 2

The first time you perform this skill you will probably pike excessively. As you progress, attempt to minimize the degree of pike as illustrated. Practice holding the front support position after the circle has been completed. Numerous skills are based on the backward hip circle; master every detail of this skill.

Basic Description

(1-2) Cast off the bar from a front support position.

(3-5) With your back slightly arched, allow hips to swing freely back to the bar. As hips approach the bar, lean shoulders backward and pike slightly; the combination of the lean and pike will initiate backward rotation. Do not throw head back as you circle the bar. Watch your toes during the first half of the circle. Your arms should bend slightly to allow you to place the bar just below hip bones. As you circle, the bar will come to

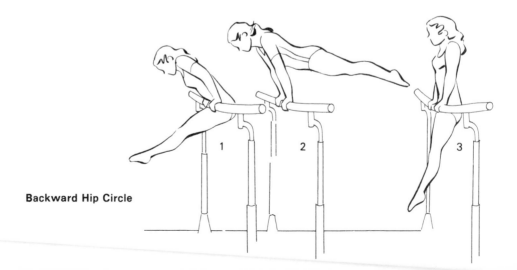

Backward Hip Circle

Cast to Handstand

rest against thighs rather than hip area; this facilitates straightening the body toward the end of rotation. As legs reach a horizontal position near the end of the circle, open from the slightly piked position by raising upper body and arching your back.

(6) Stop and hold the front support position at the end of the circle.

Prerequisites

Ability to cast off the bar in a front support position. Backward pullover mount to front support.

Spotting

Stand between the bars on the left side of performer. Place left hand under performer's thighs and right hand on her lower back as she leans back and starts the circle. Support and aid the rotation. Move hands to performer's legs to stabilize them in the front support position.

Free Backward Hip Circle (Variation)

Skill Level 6

See free backward hip circle mount under "Mounts."

Backward Hip Circle Hecht to Eagle Catch (Variation)

Skill Level 7

This is one of many skills based on the backward hip circle. The hip-lift technique (described earlier in this chapter) is used to bounce away from the low bar. This skill starts with a high cast, followed by a fast backward hip circle that allows the performer to release the bar and open from the hip circle early. A fast arching of the back provides the lift for an eagle grip catch on the high bar. This skill requires an upper body and hip spot as the lift occurs.

Backward Hip Circle Hecht to Eagle Catch

Forward Hip Circle

Skill Level 2

The forward hip circle can be used before any skill that starts from a front support position. It may also be used as a mount. In this case, the performer runs, jumps from a vaulting board with arms extended overhead, contacts the bar with her thighs while holding her body straight, and thrusts her arms downward into the hip circle. This is the only forward circling skill commonly executed with the "wrong grip"—a double over grip. In the middle of the circle the performer must release her grips and quickly reach over the top of the bar and grasp it again. This shifting of the grips allows the gymnast to hold a more stable front support position at the end of the circle.

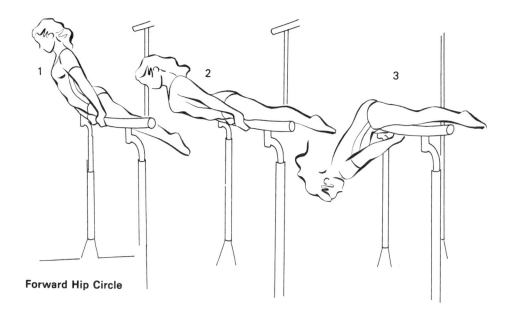

Forward Hip Circle

Basic Description

(1) Assume a front support position with over grips.

(2) Push down in your shoulders and place the bar against upper thighs, lower than usual. At the same time, lean forward (keeping body straight) with a slight forward-thrusting action.

(3) When body reaches a horizontal position, pike deeply by quickly thrusting head under the bar toward legs.

(4-5) Quickly shift grips, bringing hands over the top of the bar. The bar should not leave the hip area; however, it will "travel" slightly from upper thighs to the area just below hip bones. If you are not fast enough or do not pike deeply enough, you will either not complete the circle or finish very low on your chest. After shifting grips, push down and pull shoulders over the bar.

(6) The final position of a good forward hip circle is a piked front support position that allows you to cast off the bar with lots of power.

Prerequisites
All preceding skills are recommended.

Spotting
Stand between the bars to the left side of performer. Reach under the bar and place left hand on performer's lower back as she falls forward. Help performer gain momentum for the roll by gently pressing downward on her back. As performer pikes, transfer left hand to the back of thighs and place right hand under lower back. Shift hand positions very fast and give lots of support during the last phase of this skill.

Forward Hip Circle from Eagle Hang

Forward Hip Circle from Eagle Hang (Variation)

Skill Level 5

The performer in the illustration has just finished catching the high bar in an eagle grip after a backward hip circle on the low bar (*see* cast wrap to eagle catch). From an arched position, she lifts her legs as she swings forward, thrusting her hips toward the low bar. She then pushes off the high bar with her arms to project her body forward into the forward hip circle.

Drop to Forward Hip Circle from Stoop over High Bar

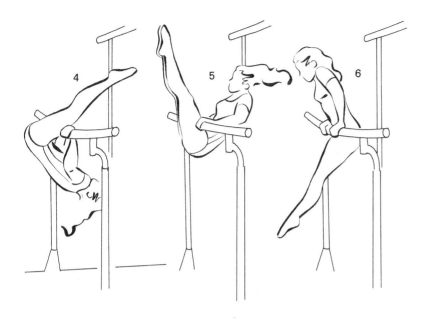

Prerequisites

All preceding skills are recommended.

Spotting

Stand between the bars to the left side of performer. Reach under the bar and place left hand on performer's lower back as she falls forward. Help performer gain momentum for the roll by gently pressing downward on her back. As performer pikes, transfer left hand to the back of thighs and place right hand under lower back. Shift hand positions very fast and give lots of support during the last phase of this skill.

Forward Hip Circle from Eagle Hang

Forward Hip Circle from Eagle Hang (Variation)

Skill Level 5

The performer in the illustration has just finished catching the high bar in an eagle grip after a backward hip circle on the low bar (*see* cast wrap to eagle catch). From an arched position, she lifts her legs as she swings forward, thrusting her hips toward the low bar. She then pushes off the high bar with her arms to project her body forward into the forward hip circle.

Drop to Forward Hip Circle from Stoop over High Bar

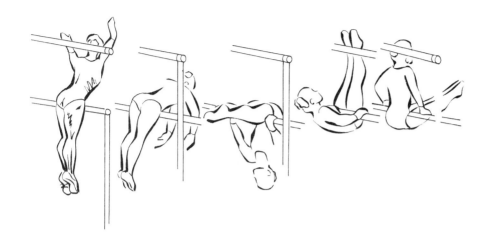

Drop to Forward Hip Circle from Stoop over High Bar (Variation)

Skill Level 6

This is a "gutsy" forward hip circle variation usually appreciated by an audience. The performer casts into a stoop over the high bar and uses her arms to guide her body into position for the free drop to the low bar. She lands, hands first, on the low bar with her body leaning slightly forward for the forward hip circle. There is a tendency to pike too much as the body hits the low bar, which makes the hip circle difficult. A spotter should support the performer's back during the circle.

Single-Leg Squat to Stride Support; Double-Leg Squat to Rear Support

Skill Levels 2 and 3

This skill may be performed with one leg or both legs passed between your arms and over the bar. Both movements can be used to simply stand on the bar if the next skill begins with a standing position.

Basic Description

(1-3) Cast from a front support position with over grips. Raise hips and depress (push down) shoulders with your arms as leg(s) passes over the bar. Quickly pass leg(s) over the bar. The shoulders move backward slightly during the leg squat to compensate for the weight of leg(s) brought forward. In performing the double-leg squat to rear support, push down with shoulders as you squat over the bar; this will give you a little more leg room. As legs move forward, shoulders must move backward to balance in a rear support.

(4) Finish in a stride support position (single-leg squat) or a rear support position (double-leg squat).

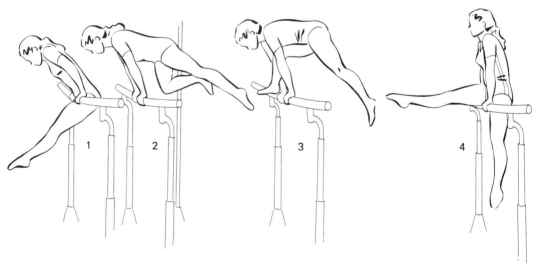

Single-Leg Squat to Stride Support

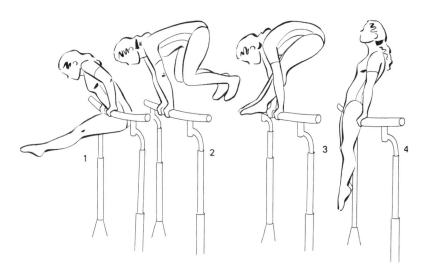

Double-Leg Squat to Rear Support

Prerequisites

Single-leg squat to a stand on the bar. Learn the single-leg squat before the double-leg squat.

Spotting

Stand on the side of performer and grasp upper arm. Stabilize arms during and after the squatting action.

Cast off High Bar to Hanging Swing

Skill Level 3

Concentrate on achieving a straight body position very soon after casting away from the bar. Get assistance from a good spotter while learning this skill. Have the spotter support your body during several casts from the low bar to be sure you are able to hold your body straight. If a strong jerk occurs at the bottom of the swing, you could slip off. This is a very important movement that is used quite often, so take your time and learn it well. To pick up a slight swing, push off the low bar with your feet while hanging on the high bar. After you push off, extend your body to the rear and swing back and forth a couple of times. Your spotter can push you into this swing also. Be careful not to hit the low bar too hard; if you do, pike as you hit it to absorb the shock. This tactic transfers most of the energy of the swing to your legs, preventing too much jarring of the hips. Use a padded bar if this skill hurts your hip bones.

The correct width of the bars should be determined by swinging from a stretched hang into a piked position against the low bar. The width is proper if the low bar touches your hips and allows you to achieve a maximum piked position.

Basic Description

(1-3) From a front support on the high bar, execute a *flat* (horizontal) cast. *Straighten arms* with a smooth push so that you don't jerk at the bottom of the swing. Hold body straight and keep upper arms and upper body in a straight line during the descent.

(4-5) Swing forward toward the low bar with body straight (even a slight pike may hurt your hip bones). As you hit the low bar, absorb the shock by piking.

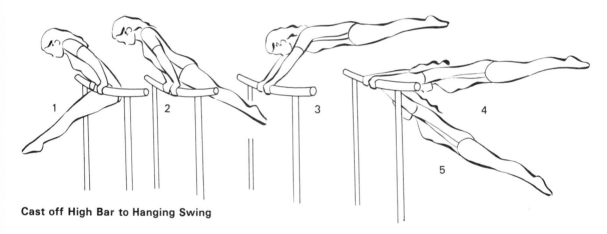

Cast off High Bar to Hanging Swing

Prerequisites

All preceding skills are recommended.

Spotting

Stand on piled-up mats underneath the high bar to the left side of performer. As performer casts, reach up and put right hand on her thighs and left hand on her stomach. Guide performer through the swing, lowering her rather slowly until she can perform a smooth swing on her own.

Cast off High Bar to Backward Hip Circle on Low Bar (Cast Wrap)

Skill Level 4

This skill must be spotted during the learning stage. The width of the bars must be adjusted for each performer. Test the width by swinging and piking as you hit the bar. The bar should fit right into the area between your hip bones and your upper thighs. If your swing to the low bar is stretched, you will have little difficulty learning this skill. You will gain confidence as you feel the "hugging" sensation the bar gives you as your legs move into the piked position.

Basic Description

(1-3) Execute a smooth, stretched cast to a swing below the high bar. (*See* cast off high bar to hanging swing.)

(4) As hips approach the low bar, they should be straight or slightly arched.

(5) As hips touch the low bar, pike with a smooth movement. Keep eyes focused on legs as the pike occurs. The bar should hit hips just below hip bones.

(6) Release the high bar as legs pass beyond a vertical position. The piking action should press you to the bar.

(7-8) Move hands to the low bar, grasp it with over grips, and raise upper body

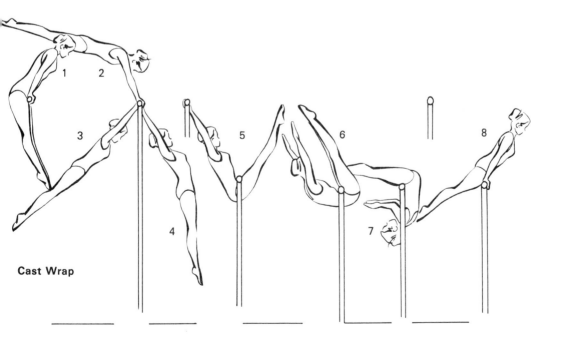

Cast Wrap

into an arched position. If you allow legs to rotate beyond a horizontal position prior to the arch, you will probably over-rotate the backward hip circle and finish standing on the floor.

Prerequisites
Backward hip circle. Cast to swing from the high bar. All preceding skills are recommended.

Spotting
Follow the cast to a hang without interfering with the swing. Spot the backward hip circle as described earlier. The spotter must move quickly to keep up with performer and be ready to catch her at any point during the circle.

Cast Wrap to Eagle Catch

Skill Level 6

This series can be performed with a half turn to a catch with mixed grips, to a catch with double under grip, to a glide on the low bar, and with hecht dismounts. All of these skills require a "popping" movement off the low bar.

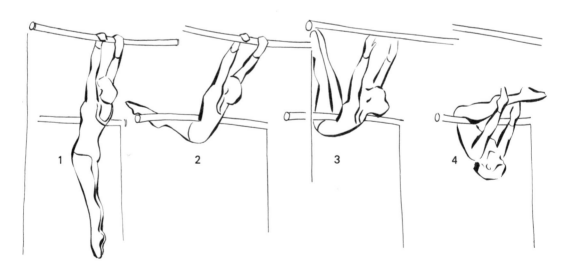

Cast Wrap to Eagle Catch

Basic Description

(1-4) Execute a cast off the high bar to a backward hip circle as described earlier. The three major differences between the opening (straightening the body) for the eagle catch and the opening for a plain front support are the timing of the opening, the speed of the opening, and the position of the arms.

(5-6) Begin opening when legs *approach* a vertical position near the end of the circle. Lift arms overhead forcefully, raise upper body, tighten seat muscles, and thrust heels upward into an arched body position. The opening from the pike into the arch is so aggressive that it "pops" you upward and backward off the bar.

(7-9) As arms move overhead, turn wrists and shoulders outward, reach for the high bar, and grasp it with an eagle grip. Your arms should be wide enough apart to accommodate your degree of shoulder flexibility; if arms are spread too wide, you will miss the bar. If your timing is correct and you still miss the bar, it is probably because you are not arching heels and upper body forcefully and/or reaching too wide. The illustration shows a preliminary swing resulting from a cast half turn on the high bar; hence the mixed grips.

Prerequisites

All preceding casting and backward hip circle skills. Eagle grip hang. Complete control of the "popping" movement of a hip-lift off the low bar.

Spotting

Hold performer's legs as she hangs over the low bar in a piked position. Have her arch on command as you lift her to the high bar. Repeat this drill until she learns to open aggressively from the piked position. Two spotters may be used initially if performer is above average in size. One spotter catches performer's upper body and the other holds legs up. A single spotter should spot the first phase by following the procedure used in spotting the cast from the high bar. As performer's legs are brought over the bar and down at the end of the circle, grasp upper back area from the side, and guide and lift. Do not grab only performer's legs because the rest of her may continue flying over the top and away.

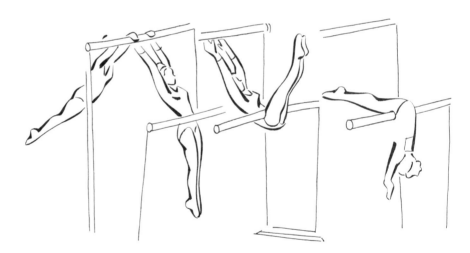

Cast Wrap Half Turn to Catch

Cast Wrap Half Turn to Catch (Variation)

Skill Level 6

The timing of the opening of the half-turn catch is similar to the timing of the eagle grip catch. The half-turn movement is initiated as part of the opening from the piked position; however, the body must be fully arched for a forceful "pop" off the bar. Many beginners become too concerned with the turn-and-catch and fail to finish the lifting phase. Grasp the high bar with your leading hand as you turn. You may finish with over grips or crossed grips if you wish to continue turning.

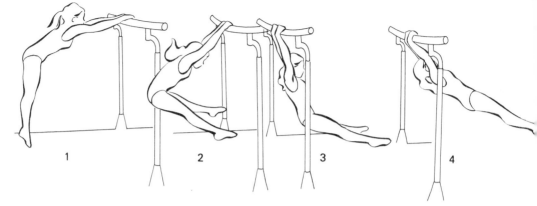

1   2   3   4

Glide to Single-Leg Overshoot

Glide to Single-Leg Overshoot

Skill Level 4

This is a rather difficult basic skill. The secret is to get your top leg between your arms quickly while allowing your body to rotate slightly backward.

Basic Description
  (1) Jump to a glide swing with legs straddled or together. As hands contact the bar, upper arms and upper body should form a straight line. Do not pike excessively; this will cause legs to drop toward the end of the swing. Pike just enough to keep feet off the floor throughout the glide.
  (2-4) Swing forward to a position of full extension in shoulders and hips.
  (5-6) Quickly lift legs upward toward the bar while splitting them. A special effort must be made to bring overshoot leg close to chest between arms. This movement must be very fast; otherwise, the swing will be dead by the time leg is in position to be thrust upward.
  (7-9) Keep your shooting leg away from the bar. Pull down with arms and shoot leg up rather than forward. Keep upper body fairly straight; if you round your back and lean forward in an effort to pull yourself over the bar, you will probably hit the bar with your top leg. Finish in a stride support position.

Prerequisites
A good glide swing. Forward stride circle.

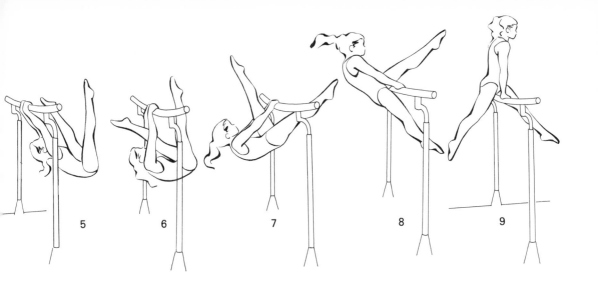

5   6   7   8   9

Spotting

Stand between the bars on performer's left side if she overshoots with her left leg. Follow the glide by squatting under the low bar. Place hands on performer's lower back and help her rise. The overshoot leg may have to be guided during the last phase.

Glide Kip

Skill Level 6

The glide kip gives many beginning gymnasts a hard time because it requires strong hip flexor muscles and considerable arm-pulling power. Be sure you can execute the ankles-to-the-bar movement with your legs straight and also with your knees bent. You cannot loaf in performing this skill; a well-timed, dynamic effort is necessary to get above the bar from the glide position.

Most problems with glide movements are the result of a late recovery from the glide; bringing your legs up to the bar fast takes lots of hard training. The ability to execute a glide kip usually marks the transition from elementary to intermediate performance on the uneven parallel bars. Above-average strength and coordination are required for this skill.

Glide Kip

Basic Description

    (1) Glide as you would in a glide to a single-leg overshoot. As you stretch forward at the end of the swing, elevate hips by pressing them upward.

    (2) Quickly bring ankles to the bar before shoulders return to an under-the-bar position. Most beginners are too slow with this movement. Do not throw head back as you bring feet to the bar because it will retard your leg lift.

(3-5) Shoot legs along the bar (not downward) without touching the bar. Simultaneously pull down toward hips with straight arms. Your objective is to get shoulders over the bar, so think of the arm-pull as a means of doing just that.

    (6) A good kip leaves you in a support position with a slight pike so that you can immediately cast into any skill that begins with the front support position.

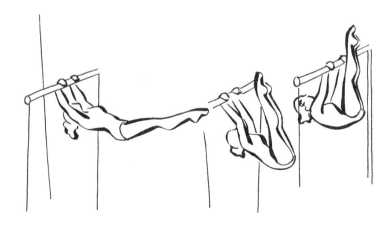

Glide Kip and Catch High Bar

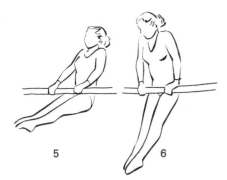

5   6

Prerequisites

A good glide swing. Ability to do straight-leg raises from a hang. Most of the preceding skills are recommended.

Spotting

Stand behind the bar to the left side of performer. Squat down and help her lift legs to the bar with your left hand. Place right hand on performer's lower back and assist with the arm-pulling phase.

Glide Kip and Catch High Bar (Variation)

Skill Level 6

The glide kip to a catch is almost the same as the glide kip. The difference is that the legs do not have to be brought up to the bar quite as fast, and there

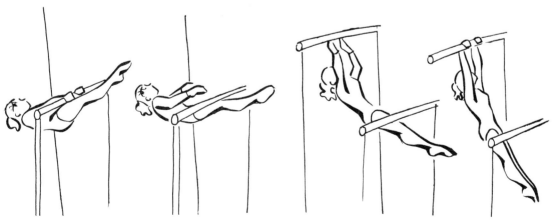

is no follow-through with the kipping action; you simply shoot your legs and pull shoulders upward rather than over the bar, then release the low bar and grasp the high bar. The spotter should stand behind performer and lift after the release. Learn the glide kip first.

Kip to High Bar from Rear Support Hang

Skill Level 5

From a rear support hang, vigorously arch back and thrust shoulders forward. Quickly bring legs to the high bar a moment before your shoulders drop below your hands. Shoot legs along the bar and pull shoulders over the bar with straight arms.

Glide to Double-Leg Overshoot

Skill Level 6

This skill is similar to a glide to a single-leg overshoot, and to a kip. The last phase should be practiced separately: Sit on the bar, drop backward into a piked swing, and shoot back over bar on the return swing. Have a spotter assist you during both parts of this skill. *See* instructions for swinging in a piked inverted hang earlier in this chapter.

Basic Description
(1-3) Glide as you would for a glide to a single-leg overshoot.
   (4) Quickly bring legs between arms with a slight backward rotation of upper body. This should be accomplished before shoulders return to the bottom of the swing. For one moment you should be in a maximum piked position under the bar.

Glide to Double-Leg Overshoot

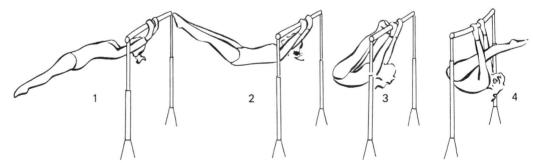

(5-6) Shoot legs upward and pull down on the bar with shoulders raised. Your legs should not touch the bar. Most beginners shoot legs into the bar, stopping the swing, and allow upper body to fall backward, resulting in no downward arm pull. Concentrate on keeping shoulders moving upward as legs shoot over the bar in the final phase. Your ability to do this is dependent upon an early inverted stoop between hands, which promotes swing and early control in the final phase.

(7) Finish in a rear support position, or grasp the high bar as your seat touches the low bar.

Prerequisites

A good glide to a single-leg overshoot. Ability to swing in a piked inverted hang.

Spotting

See glide to single-leg overshoot and glide kip.

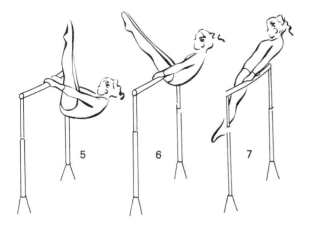

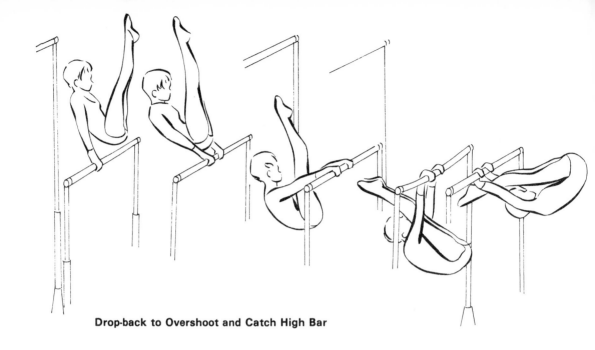

Drop-back to Overshoot and Catch High Bar

Drop-back to Overshoot and Catch High Bar (Variation)

Skill Level 4

This overshoot movement is similar to that of the glide to a double-leg over-shoot and features a piked inverted hang. The grip change to the high bar may also be executed from a glide swing. The drop-back off the bar at the start is performed by raising your hips and legs to a "V" position and pulling your seat downward as you lean backward off-balance. Maximum piking is achieved at the bottom of the swing as the lower calf area passes the bar. On the return swing, shoot legs upward and pull down with arms to elevate shoulders. As you feel your body moving over the low bar, release the low bar and quickly catch the high bar.

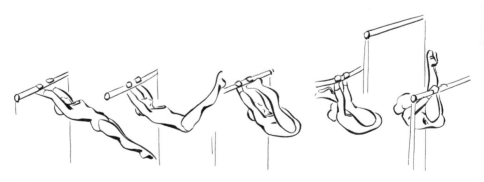

Glide to Overshoot and Catch High Bar

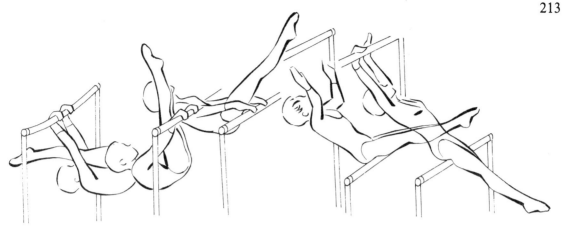

Glide to Overshoot and Catch High Bar (Variation)

Skill Level 6

The performer in this illustration demonstrates unusual control after the over-shoot. The performer takes her time changing her grips to the high bar even though her body is not balanced on the low bar; she is relying on the force of her overshoot to keep her shoulders moving upward as she transfers her grips.

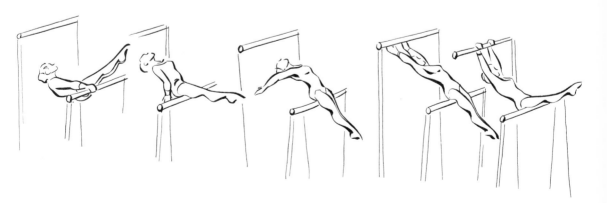

Glide to Back Kip

Skill Level 7

The back kip, closely related to the backward seat circle, should be learned on the low bar so that you can easily jump forward off the bar to a stand if you miss. As the performer passes the bottom of the swing, the bar is held about midway between the seat and the knees. As the upper body is raised sharply, the lower seat area is brought against the bar and the grips are shifted to the top of the bar for support. After the opening from the pike begins, the head and shoulders never stop moving upward until the rear support is achieved.

The grip shift should be practiced separately: Stand with your back to a bar that is about lower back level and practice jumping backward to a rear support, turning your wrists from under to over the bar during the jump. Use over grips with your hands behind you.

Also practice swinging back and forth under the bar in a piked inverted hang position. This movement requires a hip thrust as you swing backward under the bar and a leg-shooting motion as you swing forward. A spotter should help you swing in this position.

Finally, try a third drill. As you swing down to begin circling the bar, try to accelerate the swing by leading with your hips. Just before the end of the swing, raise your upper body and shift your grips quickly. Try to finish in an arched rear support. Your spotter should hold your legs for stability as you

Glide to Back Kip

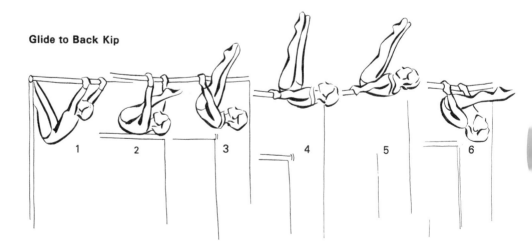

1   2   3   4   5   6

open to the arched position. Some gymnasts think that this drill is more difficult than the skill itself.

Basic Description
(1-5) Perform a glide swing as you would for a single-leg overshoot. Execute a double-leg overshoot movement but stop short of the rear support phase. The legs shoot straight up and shoulders rise to bar level.

(6-10) Forcefully pull hips downward into a deep piked position and keep legs away from the bar. After shoulders *pass* the bottom, raise upper body quickly. Shift grips to an over-the-bar grasp as you open to a sitting position.

Prerequisites
Rocking under the bar in a piked inverted hang. Glide to a double-leg over-shoot. Backward seat circle.

Spotting
Stand in front of the low bar on performer's left side. As performer opens from the pike in the last phase, put left hand on her stomach and right hand around near leg just below knee. Give performer support so that she can shift grips and lean back on the bar. (Always insist that performer finish the final, arched rear support phase.)

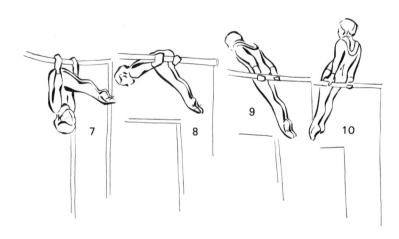

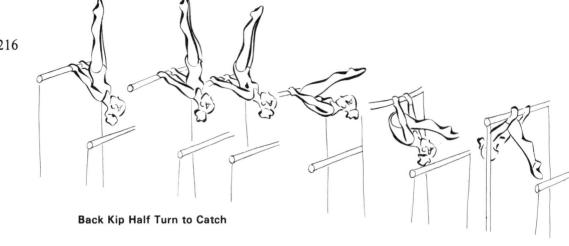

Back Kip Half Turn to Catch

Back Kip Half Turn to Catch (Variation)

Skill Level 8

Learn this skill on the low bar first. Follow all of the instructions for the back kip. Soon after the opening from the pike is initiated (elevation of shoulders), release right hand and turn left. Your upward swing continues for a brief moment as you turn. Release left hand and catch the bar.

Hang and Drop to Glide

Skill Level 4

This skill requires fast hands and strong hip muscles for the glide that usually follows. The hang drop is often used after a cast wrap to an eagle catch or a kip catch. It enables you to switch bars quickly and go directly into a glide skill. You may start with any grip combination.

Basic Description
(1) Jump to a hang on the high bar with any of the grip combinations. Beginners should use an over grip.
(2-3) Arch your back by driving heels backward and thrusting shoulders forward; this action will pull upper body slightly forward. Release the bar.
(4) Raise hips for glide position as you reach for the low bar. Catch the low bar and glide.

Hang and Drop to Glide

Prerequisites
Practice the drop to a stand until you are ready to glide. Glide skills.

Spotting
Hold performer's hips in the correct position for a glide as the drop occurs.

Hang Half-Turn Drop to Glide

Skill Level 4

Practice the turn using various grips so that you can feel the difference in the hand-pulling movement with each.

Basic Description

    (1) Hang facing away from the low bar with an over grip, under grip, eagle grip, or mixed grip. Arch your back by driving heels backward and shoulders forward.

  (2-3) Pike into a push off the high bar and into a turn. This is a jerking motion that leaves you suspended for an instant. Keep hips straight during the turn.

  (4-5) After the turn, raise hips for the glide swing. Catch the low bar and glide.

Hang Half-Turn Drop to Glide

Prerequisites

Glide skills. Practice the half turn from the high bar, dropping to a stand on a mat.

Spotting

Stand on the side of performer opposite the direction of the turn. Hold performer's waist with both hands. Lift and support the turn, and support the drop.

Backward Seat Circle

Skill Level 5

The backward seat circle is usually taught before the back kip because it is less complicated—it is the last part of the back kip. The only difference is that the backward seat circle starts from a rear support, while the last phase of the back kip begins short of this position. The grip shift takes place near the end of the circle. The bar is midway between the seat and knees at the bottom of the swing.

Basic Description

(1-6) Raise legs to a vertical piked position and pull hips straight down away from the bar. This movement will help you avoid the common mistake of turning over backward too much during the drop. This skill may also be performed in a closed piked position throughout. In this case, pump your seat throughout the last phase in a tight piked position until you arrive at a free "L" rear support position.

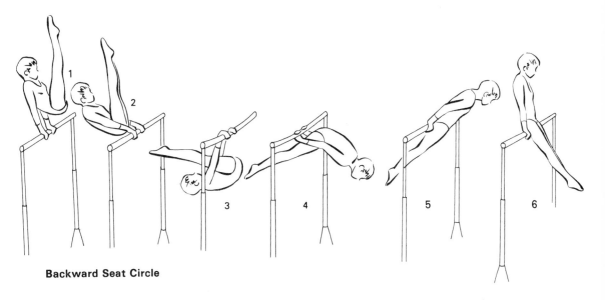

Backward Seat Circle

Prerequisites
Perform the lead-up drills for the back kip.

Spotting
See back kip.

Backward Seat Circle Half Turn to Front Support Hang

Backward Seat Circle Half Turn to Front Support Hang (Variation)

Skill Level 8

The back kip half turn to catch is the prerequisite for this skill. Practice on the low bar with a spotter catching your legs after the turn. When you practice on the high bar, be sure the low bar is padded. The spotter should stand on an elevated platform and catch the performer as she turns.

Backward Seat Circle to Stand on Low Bar

Backward Seat Circle to Stand on Low Bar (Variation)

Skill Level 7

See backward seat circle. Practice this skill on the low bar with a simulated lower bar (mats) placed in the same relationship to the low bar as that of the low bar to the high bar. There is slightly more hip lead in this seat circle prior to shifting the grips. The performer is able to watch the low bar prior to the stand.

Forward Seat Circle

Skill Level 5

Keep your head in a neutral position throughout the circle. If you throw your head backward, it will tend to keep you from elevating your shoulders during the last phase of this skill.

Basic Description

(1-3) Assume a sitting position on the bar with a double under grip. Raise the backs of your thighs off the bar in an "L" position by bearing down with arms and shoulders. Raise hips upward in the rear and close your piked position. Lean forward off-balance and direct legs downward.

(4-6) Extend hips and pull downward with arms as shoulders rise to the bar level. Do not let legs touch the bar as you open your hip angle. Beginners

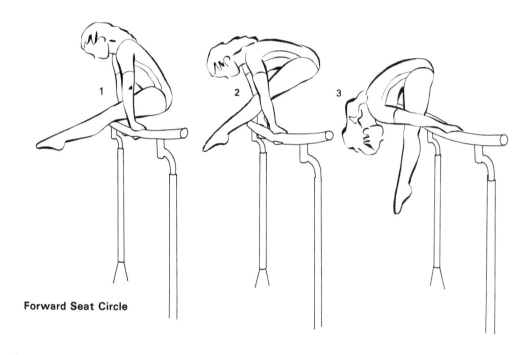

Forward Seat Circle

tend to rotate too far forward as they pass the bottom of the circle. Avoid this by extending hips a split-second late and by not rushing to get over the bar. Keep thigh muscles tight throughout.

Prerequisite
Glide to a double-leg overshoot.

Spotting
Stand between the bars and on the left side of performer. Grasp performer's wrist by reaching under the bar with left hand, thumb down, and hold wrist to the bar during the circle. Reach under performer's lower back with right forearm during the opening phase and provide support. The left hand quickly moves under the bar and grasps performer's legs to prevent over-rotation.

Forward Seat Circle Half Turn to Front Support

Forward Seat Circle Half Turn to Front Support (Variation)

Skill Level 6

This forward seat circle skill requires both a slightly earlier opening than the regular forward seat circle and a higher and more forceful leg shoot. The turn is initiated as the shoulders approach bar level in the last phase and should be directed over the support hand.

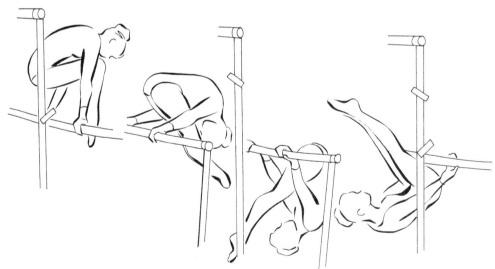

Forward Seat Circle Hop and Catch High Bar

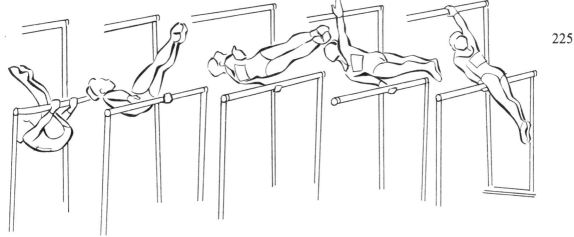

Forward Seat Circle Hop and Catch High Bar (Variation)

Skill Level 9

In the illustration, this skill is executed from a squat forward between both arms. The leg shoot is directed slightly backward as well as upward. The head must be held in a neutral position so that the high bar can be observed throughout. Spot by supporting the gymnast's back from release to catch.

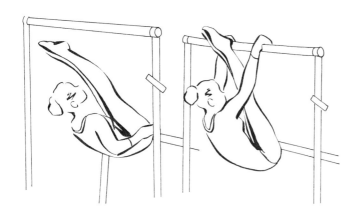

Stoop Hop Change

Stoop Hop Change; Straddle Hop Change

Skill Level 6

Follow the same basic procedure for both the stoop and straddle hop changes. Practice the bar change by shooting your legs forward to a stand on the mat without trying to catch the high bar. When you feel able to make the catch, have a spotter support your back as you release and catch. Learn a plain catch before trying the half-turn catch illustrated here. The turn is added by turning the hips near the end of the shoot phase.

Basic Description

(1) Assume a front support position. Cast to either a stoop or straddle stand on the bar. Your straddle should be a slight one on the balls of your feet.
(2) Stretch away from the bar in the shoulders and push backward off-balance.
(3) Try to pump or lead with hips as you pass the bottom of the swing.
(4) Take feet off the bar as hips move forward-upward and shoot them upward just under the high bar.

(5-7) Release the low bar and quickly reach for the high bar. Keep eyes on the high bar during the change.

Prerequisite
Undercast from a straddle circle with an aggressive leg shoot.

Spotting
Stand between the bars and to the left of performer. Hold performer's left upper arm for stability as she straddles on the bar. Release performer's left upper arm to allow her to descend. Place left hand under her seat and right hand under lower back as she passes the bottom of the swing. Avoid being kicked by performer's left leg. Guide performer to the high bar for the catch.

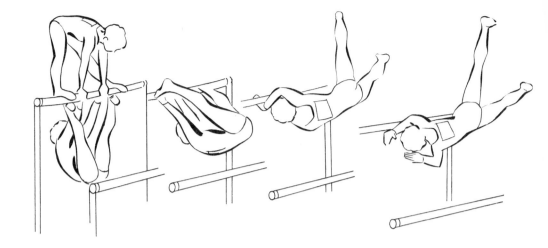

Straddle Stand and Cast Half Turn to Low Bar

Straddle Stand and Cast Half Turn to Low Bar (Variation)

Skill Level 7

Practice a plain cast over the lower bar to the mat from a straddle circle before trying a turn. A spotter should stand between the bars and support your back as you pass over the low bar. Proceed to casting with a half turn over the low bar to a stand. Finally, practice catching the low bar before you stand. The prerequisites are a good cast half turn and a glide kip.

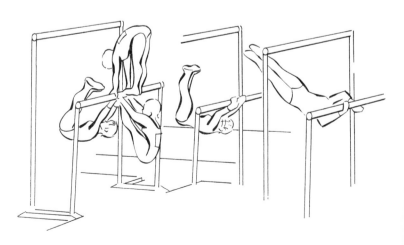

Stoop Stand and Cast Half Turn to Glide

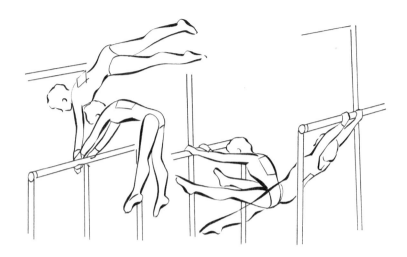

Stoop Stand and Cast Half Turn to Glide (Variation)

Skill Level 7

This skill requires good swing and a strong leg-shooting action. The shoot must be high enough to allow a half turn that finishes with the shoulders higher than the low bar. This movement should be mastered to a stand before proceeding to a glide.

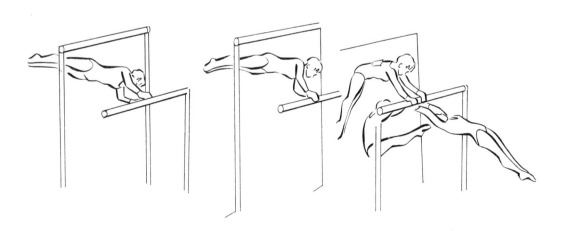

Mounts begin from a standing position or with a run and jump, usually off a vaulting board. To insure consistency, your steps must be counted, you must always begin the run with the same foot, and the running distance must be measured. This procedure will allow you to concentrate on the jump and the bar in front of you. *Almost any skill that begins from a front support or a hang can be used as a mount.* Simply jump to that position and start your exercise. You cannot make a mount out of a skill based on a front support on the *high bar* because it is impossible to jump to that position from the floor.

Following are some common mounts. Learn mounts that get you off to a confident start.

Straddle or Squat over Low Bar and Catch High Bar Mount

Skill Level 5

Practice this mount by performing a straddle or squat jump onto a broad surface such as a trampoline. Try to reach for a make-believe bar before your feet touch the surface of the trampoline. You can also use a vaulting horse, but be sure to land on several mats.

Basic Description
(1-4) Run and jump off the board. Grasp the bar with a double over grip. Push down forcefully as you raise hips and straddle or squat over the bar. Your upper body should be in a fairly erect position.
(5-8) When you are sure that your feet have cleared the bar or will clear the bar, look and reach for the high bar, using the correct grip for the next skill.

Prerequisite
Ability to consistently straddle- or squat-vault over something as high as the low bar.

Spotting
Stand in front of performer, catch her waist, and guide her over the bar while stepping backward.

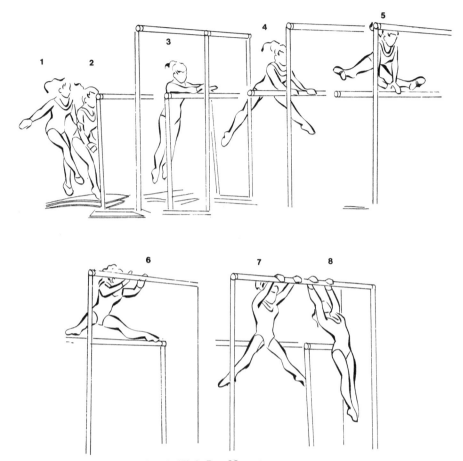

Straddle over Low Bar and Catch High Bar Mount

Free Forward Hip Circle Mount

Skill Level 3

Many beginners start piking too early as they leave the vaulting board. There is also a tendency to land on the bar with the stomach rather than the upper thighs.

Basic Description

(1-3) Run and jump off the board with arms held upward. Contact the bar on upper thigh area with body held straight at about a forty-five-degree angle. Fall forward until body reaches a horizontal position; then drive arms downward under the bar toward legs in a deep piked position.

(4-6) Grasp the bar with a double over grip and push downward to get shoulders over the bar. You should be slightly piked when you recover so that you can immediately cast into your next skill. *See* forward hip circle.

Free Forward Hip Circle Mount

Prerequisites

Forward hip circle. Forward hip circle without using your arms for the first phase.

Spotting

Stand in front of the low bar and on the left side of performer. After the pike occurs, support lower back and the backs of thighs. This mount is rather "gutsy," so spotter should give performer confidence with lots of physical support.

Free Backward Hip Circle Mount

Skill Level 6

This skill is often taught on the men's low horizontal bar because the smaller bar affords better hand control.

Basic Description

(1) Run and jump to a high free front support.

(2-3) Lower toward the bar with a slightly rounded body. When hips are about eight inches from the bar, pike slightly and lean backward with head held in a neutral position and eyes focused on legs. The speed of the circle during its first phase is very important in performing free backward hip circles. To increase speed, lean backward off-balance, before the pike occurs, with feet held behind hips (straight body drop). As body descends in this position, pike slightly to increase rotation.

(4-5) Continue piking as body descends. Pike only enough to lightly touch upper legs to the bar just above the kneecaps as shoulders pass through the bottom of the circle. If your body is tight and your swing is aggressive, the bar will flex deeply at this point.

(6-8) Open your pike to a straight body position by extending hips and pulling with *straight arms,* simultaneously shifting your grips from under the bar to an over-the-bar position. Continue pushing as you thrust your body to a free front support or to a handstand.

Free Backward Hip Circle Mount

Prerequisites

Backward hip circle. Free backward hip circle is recommended before practicing the rise to a handstand.

Spotting

Stand to the left of performer as she jumps. As she descends below the bar, place right hand on upper back or shoulder and left hand under lower back. Try to position performer by aiding the circle and the leg-shoot. If it is handled correctly, a slight shoulder boost will help performer shoot legs and shift grips. Catch performer's thighs and hold them in place after body opens from the pike.

Half Turn to Kip Mount

Skill Level 7

Try this mount on the low bar before proceeding to the high bar. Instead of a two-foot jump, step into the jump-turn.

Basic Description

(1-3) Run and jump from the board, lifting arms upward in a turning movement.

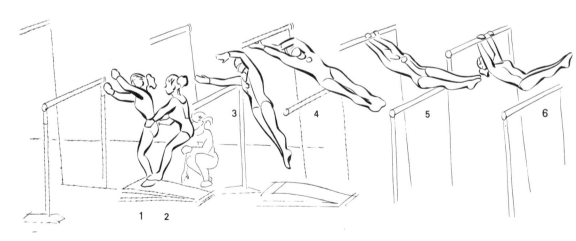

Half Turn to Kip Mount

(4-5) Turn head early so that you can see the bar before you catch. Keep body straight during the jump, which should be rather flat to enable you to catch with shoulders well in front of hands. If you pike excessively, and catch with shoulders under hands, you will not be able to kip.

(6-11) Execute the kip (*see* glide kip).

Prerequisite
Glide kip.

Spotting
Stand in front of the bars and to the side of performer. The half turn should be performed into spotter's arms for support. Spot the kip.

Piked Forward Handspring Mount

Skill Level 8

This skill may also be executed in the middle of a routine from a front support position, with performer either facing the high bar or facing away from the high bar (gainer style). It is often followed by a half-turn drop to the low bar as illustrated.

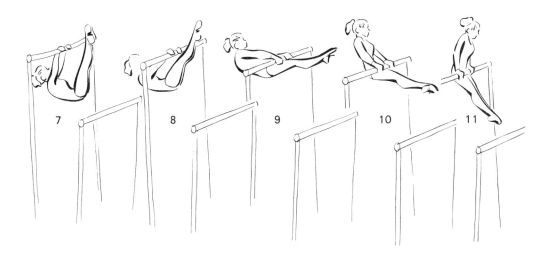

Basic Description

(1-4) Run and jump from the vaulting board. Push down on the bar and raise hips as you pull shoulders past the bar. Straddle legs early after the jump to facilitate rotation.

(5-12) Release the bar and duck head toward stomach. Reach between legs for the high bar and catch in a straddle piked inverted hang.

Piked Forward Handspring Mount

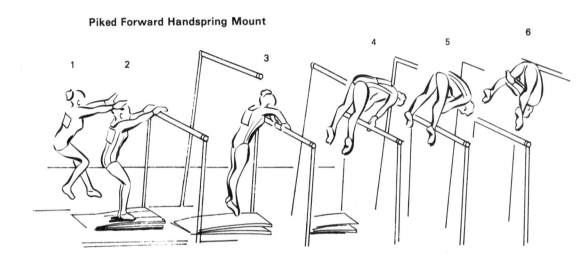

Prerequisites

At first, practice this skill to a landing on a trampoline or high crash mat instead of catching the high bar. Ability to jump to a near-handstand position on the low bar with legs straddled.

Spotting

Practice the spotting technique with performer on a crash mat. Two spotters should be used if one spotter seems inadequate. Stand between the bars, grasp performer's closest upper arm with one hand before she releases, and support her upper back with other hand. The hand that holds upper arm should move with the arm as it reaches for the bar. Step in close and get your shoulder under performer as she reaches for the high bar; you may have to support all of her weight.

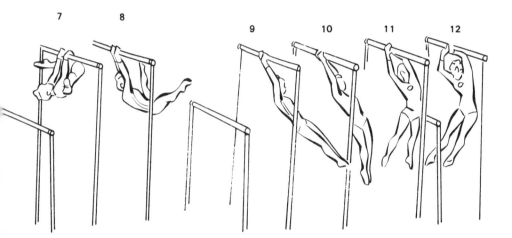

DISMOUNTS

A dismount on the uneven parallel bars is a skill or short series of skills used to end a routine. Watch the mat during dismounts so that you will know where to place your feet for the landing. The performer should always land on the mat in a standing position, bending the knees and hips to absorb the impact. Learn dismounts that are similar to some of the skills that you execute well. Take into consideration how tired you will be at the end of your routine. Also keep in mind that a dismount that scares you will probably inhibit your performance of the skills that precede it because you will be worried throughout the routine.

Single-Leg Quarter Turn Dismount

Skill Level 1

This dismount is appropriate for beginners if the low bar is low enough to hold until the landing. If the bar will not move low enough, pile up mats to elevate the landing area.

Basic Description

(1) Assume a stride support position, with hand that corresponds to forward leg in an under grip. Throw rear leg over the bar and execute a quarter turn toward the under grip hand.

(2-3) Join legs as early as possible and maintain a straight body position before landing.

Single-Leg Quarter Turn Dismount

Single-Leg Three-Quarter Turn Dismount (Variation)

Skill Level 1

As you descend from the bar, release support hand and grasp the bar with other hand during the three-quarter turn.

Single-Leg Three-Quarter Turn Dismount

Underswing Dismount

Skill Level 2

Watch your legs as you circle under the bar and shoot out to a stand. This skill can also be performed with a half twist and a full twist. Begin the twist as you shoot legs away from the bar.

Basic Description

(1-3) Cast off the bar from a front support position. Swing downward toward the bar with a straight body. Pike slightly and lean back as thighs approach the bar. Rotate under the bar as you increase your pike, touching the bar gently with your knees at the bottom of the circle.

Underswing Dismount

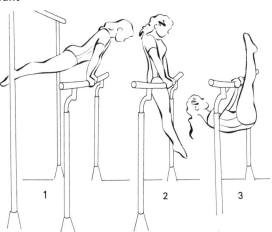

1   2   3

(4-7) Keep knees close to the bar as you lead with hips into the forward swing. Shoot legs forward-upward as you pull backward on the bar to thrust upper body forward. Bring legs under body for the landing.

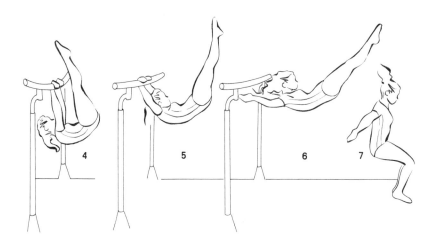

Prerequisites
Ability to cast from a front support position. Ability to hold your knees near the bar as you rotate under it.

Spotting
Stand beside performer and support lower back and legs throughout.

Straddle Stand Undercast Half Turn Dismount (Variation)

Skill Level 3

Watch the mat as you twist for the landing. *See* straddle stand and cast half turn to low bar, a related skill.

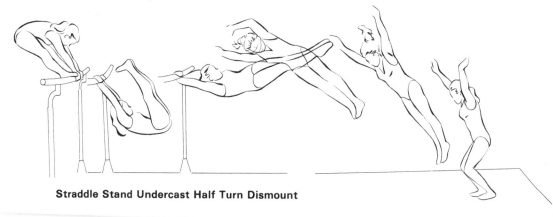

Straddle Stand Undercast Half Turn Dismount

Double-Leg Cutaway Left with Quarter Turn Left Dismount

Skill Level 4

The leg shoot and arm pull for shoulder elevation must be dynamic, or you will find yourself sagging after the turn. This dismount may be executed on the high bar after you have mastered the low bar version.

Basic Description

(1-2) Assume a rear support position. Raise thighs off the bar by bearing down with shoulders and raising legs to a "V" position. Push backward, off-balance, and pull seat downward into a tight piked swinging position. The legs move past the bar from hips to calves during underswing but do not touch the bar. Swing back up toward the starting position. Shoot legs upward and pull down on the bar until hips approach bar level.

(3-6) Release one hand and execute a quarter turn toward the released hand. Extend hips and assume a straight body position before landing. Hold on to the bar as long as possible before releasing it to land.

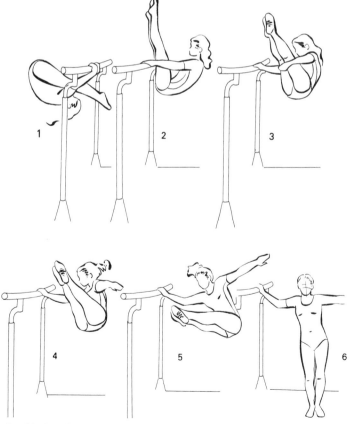

Double-Leg Cutaway Left with Quarter Turn Left Dismount

Prerequisite

Drop-back from a rear support to a piked inverted swing and overshoot to a rear support.

Spotting

Practice spotting this skill on the low bar before proceeding to the high bar. The spotter stands on the side of performer opposite the turning direction. Grasp performer's waist. Aid the turn and lift for elevation. Land performer gently.

Double-Leg Cutaway Right with Quarter Turn Left Dismount (Variation)

Skill Level 5

Learn this dismount on the low bar first. Follow the procedure for the preceding double-leg cutaway dismount, executing the left quarter turn as illustrated.

Double-Leg Cutaway Right with Quarter Turn Left Dismount

Cartwheel Dismount

Skill Level 2

The bars must be adjusted to accommodate the distance from hips to hand so that the performer can cast off the high bar.

Basic Description

(1) Assume a front support position on the high bar. Reach down and grasp the low bar with one hand, allowing legs to lower slightly as you bend forward. Your other hand grasps the high bar with an under grip.

(2-3) Cast legs overhead with a quarter turn so that you are centered directly over lower support arm. Gently push with upper support arm as legs pass through a handstand. Watch lower support arm as you cartwheel.

(4) Focus eyes on the mat as you near the landing. Bend knees slightly upon landing, and hold on to the bar for stability.

Cartwheel Dismount

Prerequisites

Control in a handstand position on the floor. Cartwheel on the floor.

Spotting

Stand on a spotting platform or elevated mats. Assist performer with the handstand position by crossing arms and holding waist with both hands. Guide and support performer to the landing.

Handstand Straddle Dismount

Skill Level 5

This dismount may also be executed from the high bar, with the performer facing in either direction.

Most beginners tend to lean forward with their shoulders rather than their hips in an attempt to make sure they clear the bar after the push. This movement should be discouraged because it shortens the range of motion for the push at the shoulders.

Other dismounts that can be performed from this starting position are the handstand arch over, handstand quarter turn, squat, and stoop dismounts.

Basic Description

(1-2) From a support position on the high bar, place hands (over grips) on the low bar. Bend hips and cast legs overhead to a controlled handstand position.

   (3) Allow legs to overbalance slightly but keep shoulders over hands. Allow lower back to sag (arch) slightly as feet pass beyond head.

   (4) Forcefully snap legs downward into a straddle position by piking from the hip and pushing downward with arms and shoulders.

(5-6) Extend body before landing. Land with feet together and knees slightly bent.

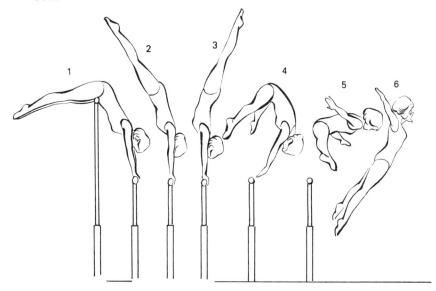

Handstand Straddle Dismount

Prerequisites

Good control in a handstand position. A good snap-down on the floor.

Spotting

This skill is best spotted by two people to insure safety and because the overbalance position should be analyzed after each attempt. Two spotters assisting from the sides can clearly observe the degree of overbalance and shoulder lean. Grasp performer's upper arm while reaching up with other hand to assist the handstand. If a second spotter is unavailable, stand in front of performer and grasp upper arms. As the snap-down occurs, pull upper arms forward and assist the landing. Avoid being hit by performer's legs during the descent. This spotting technique may also be used for a squat or stoop dismount.

Straddle Cutaway Dismount or Regrasp Bar

Skill Level 6

This skill can be used in the middle of a routine if the high bar is regrasped after the release, as illustrated. In this case, the release occurs a little later and the straddle is a little wider than in the dismount. Learn this skill as a dismount before practicing the release-and-catch. The straddle cut may be performed from a glide swing, a drop-back, or as illustrated.

Basic Description

(1-2) If you wish to start with a drop-back action instead of a rear support hang as illustrated, follow the instructions for the double-leg cutaway with quarter turn dismount.

(3-7) Shoot legs upward, pull downward with arms, and straddle legs. Release the bar as hips approach bar level and continue straddling as wide as possible. Join legs and assume a straight body position before landing.

Prerequisites

Glide to a double-leg overshoot to rear support. Drop-back to a double-leg overshoot to rear support. Ability to hold a wide straddle position.

Spotting

Stand behind performer and grasp her waist as she rises for the straddle. Provide support for the landing or a regrasp.

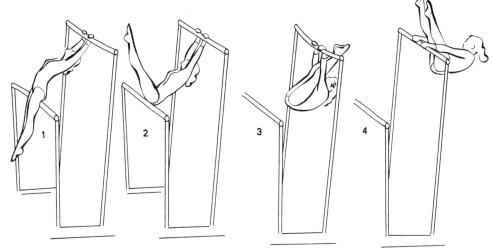

Straddle Cutaway and Regrasp Bar

Cast Wrap to Hecht Dismount

Skill Level 7

The hecht dismount may be performed with legs straddled, with a tucked backward somersault added, and with twists. With a slightly later opening from the tight piked position on the other side of the bar, you can execute a drop to a glide, a straddle to a rear support, a straddle hecht half twist catch, and many other movements. This skill should be learned with the legs straddled before it is practiced with the legs joined. After the wrap around the low bar, opening quickly from the pike and holding the body rigid maximizes the flexion of the bar, providing extra lifting power for the final phase of this dismount.

Basic Description

(1-4) Execute a cast wrap.

(5-7) When legs reach a horizontal position, quickly raise upper body and heels into an arched position with arms thrusting forward-upward. Keep hip muscles tight in the final arched position for maximum rigidity. Try to lift arms and upper body off the bar with an outward and upward reaching motion as you open the pike. Your head should remain in a neutral position throughout.

(8-11) Move arms out to the sides after hips leave the bar for increased rotation in the landing phase.

Prerequisites

Cast wrap. Cast wrap followed by some form of lifting movement off the bar.
All of the prerequisites listed for the cast wrap to eagle catch.

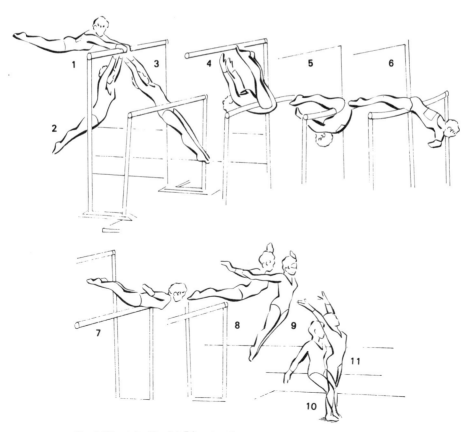

Cast Wrap to Hecht Dismount

248

Spotting

Stand to the left of performer and in front of the low bar. As she opens from the pike, very quickly put left forearm under her stomach and lift. Place right hand on her back as she leaves the bar and hold her until the landing.

Cast Wrap to Hecht Full Twist Dismount (Variation)

Skill Level 8

Follow all of the procedures for a cast wrap to a hecht dismount. The twist is initiated from the bar toward the end of the opening from the piked position. The arms are thrust upward and wide, the right arm pulling to the right to begin the twist. The right arm is then pulled close to the body and the left arm moves overhead in line with the twisting axis.

Cast Wrap to Hecht Full Twist Dismount

Spotting

Stand on the side opposite the twisting direction. Support performer's stomach as she lifts off the bar and allow her to roll on your support arm. Quickly grasp performer's waist and support the landing.

Spotting the Cast Wrap to Hecht Full Twist Dismount

Backward Hip Circle to Hecht Dismount

Skill Level 7

This skill should be learned on the low bar with legs straddled before you practice it on the high bar with legs together. The technique is basically the same for both styles. When it is done on the high bar, the gymnast may begin this dismount facing away from the low bar, which eliminates the hazard of the low bar. A full twist may be added after you master the plain hecht dismount.

Basic Description

(1-4) Execute a cast to a backward hip circle with slightly bent arms so that you can get the bar firmly embedded just below hip bones. Rotate legs vigorously under and over the bar. Watch legs as they circle.

(5-6) When legs pass a vertical position, quickly release hands from the bar and lift chest and arms aggressively. Stretch and reach forward as you open from the pike. The force of your circle and your fast opening create downward pressure on the bar. Try to feel the bar's downward flexion and rebound, and use it to aid the lift.

(7-10) Raise upper body and heels, arching with hips and lower back muscles tight. If you are limp, the bar's rebound motion will not give you a strong boost into the air. Do not throw head back at the peak of the arch. After you leave the bar, your arms may move to the sides to improve backward rotation for the landing.

Prerequisites

Backward hip circle. Cast wrap. Cast wrap to an eagle catch. Good timing and rhythm in popping off the bar from the hips.

Spotting

Stand on the left side of performer in front of the bar. As performer straightens from the hip circle, reach under her stomach with left forearm and provide support as she moves forward-upward. Hold performer all the way to the landing. Be prepared for an early opening resulting in a nose-dive.

Backward Hip Circle Quarter Turn Dismount (Variation)

Skill Level 8

See backward hip circle to hecht dismount. This dismount requires a slightly earlier opening from the piked position than a plain hecht dismount. The turn is initiated from the bar, and the left hand regrasps the bar (palm down) for support during the turn. The hip muscles are kept tight throughout the descent.

Backward Hip Circle Quarter Turn Dismount

SELECTED SKILLS AND COMBINATIONS

Just as every gymnast and coach must decide when to stop working on new skills and begin preparing a routine, an author must decide when to stop and put things together. The following skills and combinations indicate some of the possibilities on the uneven parallel bars in addition to the skills already described and illustrated.

Cast to Full Turn from Front Support Hang

Basic Description
(1) Stand on the low bar and grasp the high bar with a mixed grip. Jump backward to a wrap on the low bar.

Cast to Full Turn from Front Support Hang

(2-4) Cast legs backward-upward with hips leading into a right turn. Complete your backward cast as you start the twist. Watch the bar throughout the twisting phase. Release right hand as you twist right and look over right shoulder for the bar.

(5-7) Turn right wrist in anticipation of an over-grip catch. Release left hand and complete the full turn as you grasp the bar with right and left hands (over grips). As hips touch the low bar, pike to absorb the shock.

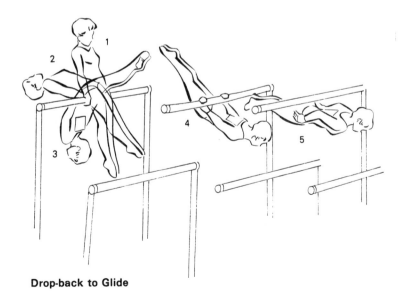

Drop-back to Glide

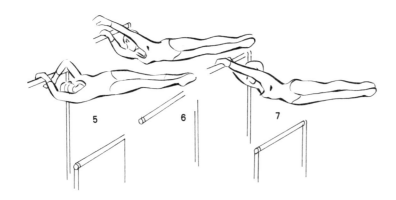

Drop-back to Glide

Basic Description

(1-4) From a rear support with the bar in the middle of your seat, arch backward with a smooth motion. The rotation should slow somewhat as you pass through the upside-down position. Keep seat muscles tight as you roll under the high bar and catch sight of the low bar.

(5-8) Release the high bar as you approach a horizontal position and grasp the low bar with hips in position for a glide swing.

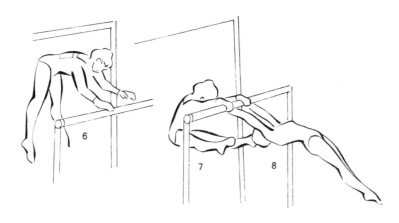

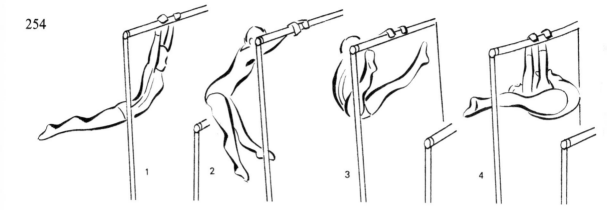

Backward Free Straddle Circle Drop to Glide

Backward Free Straddle Circle Drop to Glide

Basic Description

(1-5) From an arched swing backward on the high bar with a double over grip, quickly lift legs into a straddle piked position. When legs are pointed straight downward at the mats below, you will be able to see the low bar.

(6-8) Release the high bar a moment before the peak of the upward swing, and grasp the low bar in position for a glide swing.

Shoot to Dislocate Catch

Shoot to Dislocate Catch

Practice this skill by dropping to your stomach on piled-up crash mats after releasing the bar.

Basic Description

(1-7) Execute a drop-back to an overshoot movement. Shoot legs backward at a forty-five-degree angle as you pass the bottom of the swing.

(8-11) As your body approaches an arched position, quickly release the bar, rotate arms inward, and regrasp with over grips.

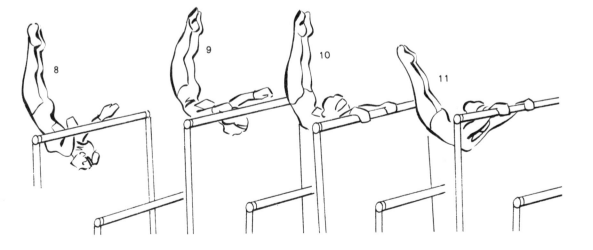

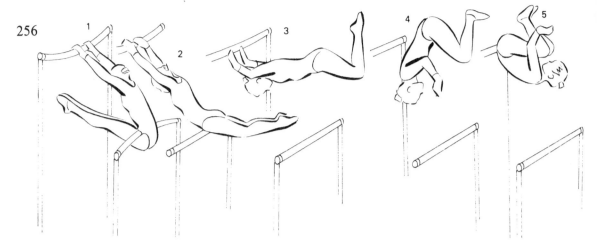

Front Support Hang and Cast to Tucked Forward Somersault Catch

Front Support Hang and Cast to Tucked Forward Somersault Catch

Use padding on the low bar, and have four spotters raise the mat between the bars to the level of the low bar as you somersault. Otherwise, use two spotters on elevated spotting platforms between the bars.

Basic Description
(1-2) Swing into a piked front support hang position. Cast legs rearward into an arch.

(3-5) Release the bar as hips continue to move upward and legs are brought toward chest into a tucked position.

(6-8) Look between your knees for the bar, and catch it.

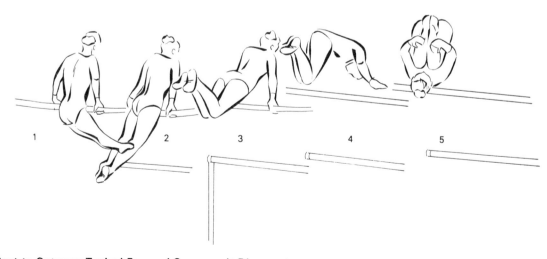

Cast to Cutaway Tucked Forward Somersault Dismount

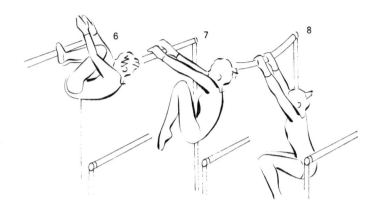

Cast to Cutaway Tucked Forward Somersault Dismount

Learn this skill on the low bar and land on crash mats.

Basic Description
(1-3) From a front support on the high bar, pike and cast to an arched position with a vigorous arm push so that shoulders move rearward behind the bar.

(4-8) Release the bar and tuck. Extend body before landing.

Jump to Back Straddle Catch from Stand on Low Bar

Jump to Back Straddle Catch from Stand on Low Bar

Practice this skill by jumping over the low bar from an elevated surface. The spotter should spot from the rear while standing on a high platform.

Basic Description
(1-5) From a stand on the low bar, jump backward, leading with hips.
(6-9) Straddle legs and grasp the bar between legs. Push away to a hang.

Back Straddle Over Low Bar from Hang on High Bar

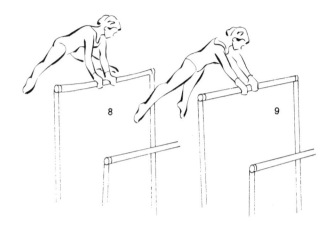

Back Straddle over Low Bar from Hang on High Bar

Spot this skill from the rear.

Basic Description

(1-3) From an arched forward swing, swing rearward and pull hips backward as you assume a straddle piked position.

(4-5) Pull down on the high bar with arms and release the bar as body moves backward over the low bar.

(6-8) Catch the low bar between legs.

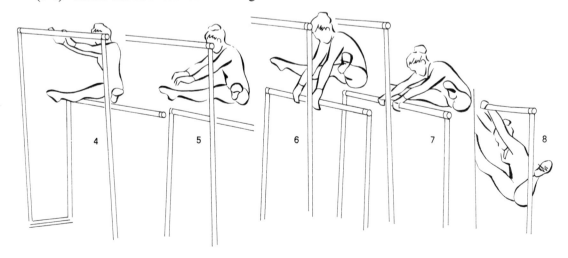

ROUTINES ON THE UNEVEN PARALLEL BARS

The following illustrations demonstrate routine composition on the uneven parallel bars. They include many skills and combinations not presented earlier.

Routine Number 1

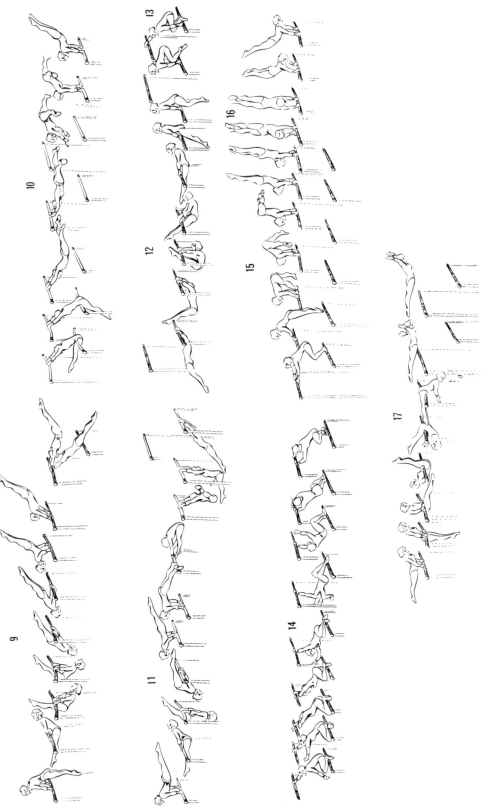

261

This routine was performed by an American national champion in 1975. The performer executes five backward hip circle skills: three free hip circles (1,9,11), one hip circle (5), and a hip circle hecht dismount (17). Although five backward hip circle skills in one routine is not ideal composition, the performer is making good use of a movement she performs extremely well. Other outstanding skills include a backward rise (4), a straddle cast half turn to support (8), a cast hop to three-quarter handstand on the low bar (10), and a handstand pirouette lower to support (15, 16).

Routine Number 2

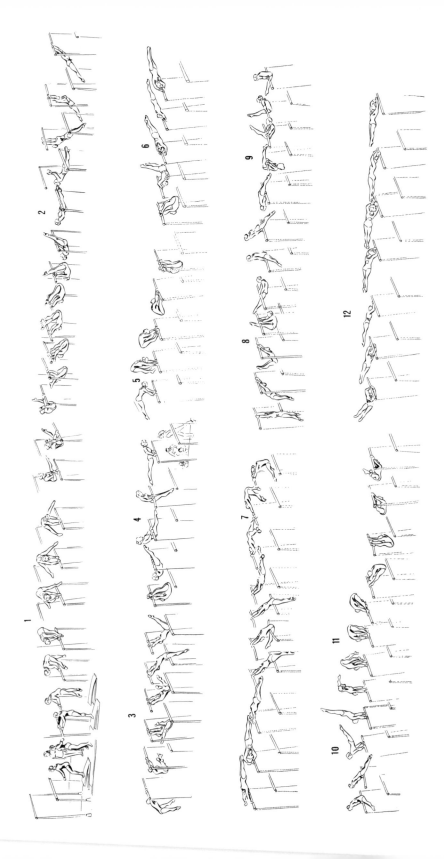

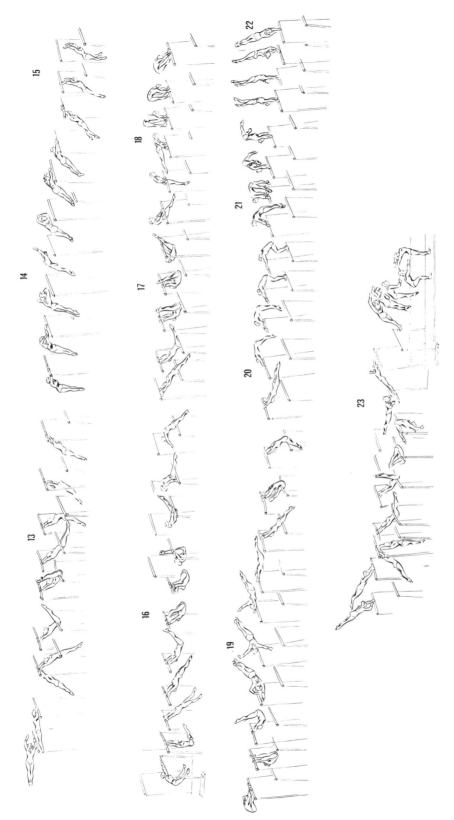

This rather long routine, performed by a Russian Olympic champion at the 1972 Olympics, features a wide variety of skills. The routine contains repetitions of the following skills: four kips (2,4,8,17), two cast one and a half turns (6,12), two handstands (10,21), and three straddle casts (5,11,18). The handstand pirouette (22) is not performed well because the turn does not finish in a near-handstand. However, the other skills in the routine are very well executed.

Routine Number 3

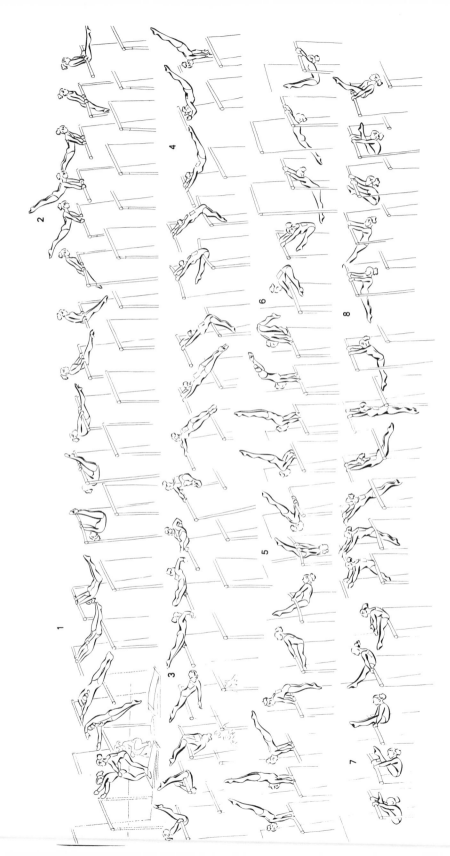

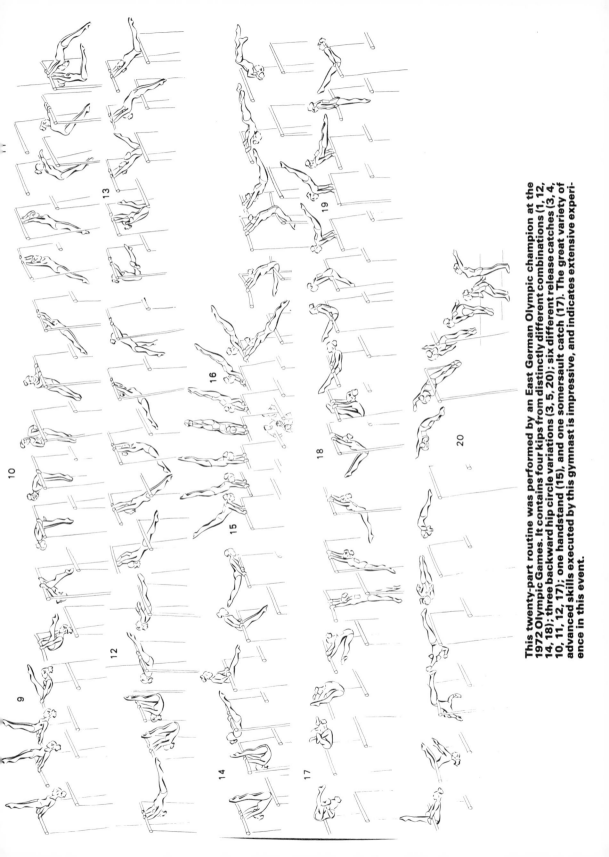

This twenty-part routine was performed by an East German Olympic champion at the 1972 Olympic Games. It contains four kips from distinctly different combinations (1, 12, 14, 18); three backward hip circle variations (3, 5, 20); six different release catches (3, 4, 10, 11, 12, 17); one handstand (15), and one somersault catch (17). The great variety of advanced skills executed by this gymnast is impressive, and indicates extensive experience in this event.